208000976

D1077028

Costs and revenues

Workbook

SHORT LOAN

David Cox

osborne
BOOKS

THE SHEFFIELD COLLEGE

The Sheffield College
City College

Accession no. 208060,976
Class 657.42 Loan category C
Date Dec 15 Price

© David Cox, 2010. Reprinted 2011.

All rights reserved. No part of this publication may be reproduced, stored in a retrieval system, or transmitted in any form or by any means, electronic, mechanical, photo-copying, recording or otherwise, without the prior consent of the copyright owners, or in accordance with the provisions of the Copyright, Designs and Patents Act 1988, or under the terms of any licence permitting limited copying issued by the Copyright Licensing Agency, Saffron House, 6-10 Kirby Street, London EC1N 8TS.

Published by Osborne Books Limited
Unit 1B Everoak Estate
Bromyard Road
Worcester WR2 5HP
Tel 01905 748071
Email books@osbornebooks.co.uk
Website www.osbornebooks.co.uk

Design by Laura Ingham
Cover and page design image © Istockphoto.com/Petrovich9

Printed by CPI Antony Rowe, Chippenham and Eastbourne

British Library Cataloguing in Publication Data
A catalogue record for this book is available from the British Library

ISBN 978 1905777 488

Contents

Acknowledgements

The publisher wishes to thank the following for their help with the reading and production of the book: Jean Cox, Maz Loton and Cathy Turner. Thanks are also due to Roger Petheram for his technical editorial work and to Laura Ingham for her designs for this series.

The publisher is indebted to the Association of Accounting Technicians for its kind permission to reproduce sample practice assessment material.

Author

David Cox has more than twenty years' experience teaching accountancy students over a wide range of levels. Formerly with the Management and Professional Studies Department at Worcester College of Technology, he now lectures on a freelance basis and carries out educational consultancy work in accountancy studies. He is author and joint author of a number of textbooks in the areas of accounting, finance and banking.

Introduction

what this book covers

This book has been written specifically to cover Learning Area 'Costs and Revenues' which combines two QCF Units in the AAT Level 3 Diploma in Accounting:

■ Principles of costing

■ Providing cost and revenue information

what this book contains

This book is set out in two sections:

■ **Chapter activities** which provide extra practice material in addition to the activities included in the Osborne Books Tutorial text. Answers to the Chapter activities are set out in this book.

■ **Practice Assessments** are included to prepare the student for the Computer Based Assessments. They are based directly on the structure, style and content of the sample assessment material provided by the AAT at www.aat.org.uk. Suggested answers to the Practice Assessments are set out in this book.

online support from Osborne Books

This book is supported by practice material available at www.osbornebooks.co.uk

This material is available to tutors – and to students at their discretion – in two forms:

■ A **Tutor Zone** which is available to tutors who have adopted the Osborne Books texts. This area of the website provides extra assessment practice material (plus answers) in addition to the activities included in this Workbook text.

■ **E-learning** – online practice questions designed to familiarise students with the style of the AAT Computer Based Assessments.

further information

If you want to know more about our products, please visit www.osbornebooks.co.uk, email books@osbornebooks.co.uk or telephone Osborne Books Customer Services on 01905 748071.

Chapter activities

1 Chapter activities
An introduction to cost accounting

1.1 Which of the following statements describe features of financial accounting and which describe features of cost accounting?

Statement	Financial accounting ✔	Cost accounting ✔
reports relate to what has happened in the past		
may be required by law		
gives estimates of costs and income for the future		
may be made public		
gives up-to-date reports which can be used for controlling the business		
is used by people outside the business		
is designed to meet the requirements of people inside the business		
shows details of the expected costs of materials, labour and expenses		
records accurate amounts, not estimates		

1.2 Which one of the following is normally classed as a fixed cost for a manufacturing business?

	✔
rent of premises	
boxes used to pack the product	
telephone costs where a charge is made for each call	
electricity metered to production machines	

1.3 Which one of the following is normally classed as a variable cost for a manufacturing business?

	✔
salary of accountant	
rent of premises	
raw materials to make the product	
insurance of machinery	

1.4 The following figures relate to the accounts of Merrett Manufacturing Limited for the year ended 31 December 20-3:

	£
Raw materials used in factory	52,170
Rent and rates of factory	8,240
Wages of production workers	73,960
Supervisors' wages	35,130
Royalties paid to designer of product	4,890
Depreciation of factory machinery	6,250
Electricity of factory	5,940
Rent and rates of office	4,290
Salaries of office staff	45,730
Depreciation of office equipment	3,750
Sundry factory expenses	2,860
Sundry office expenses	1,340
Sales revenue	286,320

You are to:

(a)   Prepare a total cost statement for the year which shows:
   •   prime cost
   •   production cost
   •   total cost

(b)   Prepare an income statement for the year (on the assumption that all the goods manufactured have been sold).

1.5 You work as an accounts assistant for Gold and Partners, an accountancy practice, which has three offices in districts of the city. The offices are at Triangle, South Toynton and St Faiths. The accounting system has been set up to show costs, revenue and money invested for each of these three offices of the practice.

The partners have requested details for each office of costs and revenue for last year, and the amount of money invested in each office at the end of the year.

The accounts supervisor asks you to deal with this request and you go to the accounts and extract the following information for last year:

	Triangle	South Toynton	St Faiths
	£000	£000	£000
Costs: materials	75	70	80
labour	550	650	730
expenses	82	69	89
Income	950	869	1,195
Money invested	750	900	1,150

The accounts supervisor asks you to present the information for the partners in the form of a report which shows the costs, profit, and return on investment (to the nearest percentage point) for each office of the practice.

1.6 Creative Clothing Limited manufactures clothes. You are to classify the company's costs into:

- direct materials
- indirect materials
- direct labour
- indirect labour
- direct expenses
- indirect expenses

The cost items to be classified are:

Cost item	Classification (write your answer)
Insurance of buildings	
Salaries of office staff	
Zip fasteners	
Electricity	
Wages of factory supervisors	
Pay of machine operators	
Consignment of blue denim cloth	
Stationery for the office	
Television advertising	
Oil for production machines	
Fuel for delivery vans	
Wages of canteen staff	

If you believe alternative classifications exist, argue the case and state if you need further information from the company.

1.7 Bunbury Buildings Limited makes garages and garden sheds which are pre-fabricated as a 'flat pack' in the factory to customer specifications.

You are working in the costing section of Bunbury Buildings and are asked to analyse the following cost items into the appropriate column and to agree the totals:

Cost item	Total cost	Prime cost	Production overheads	Admin-istration costs	Selling and distribution costs
	£	£	£	£	£
Wages of employees working on pre-fabrication line	19,205				
Supervisors' salaries	5,603				
Materials for making pre-fabricated panels	10,847				
Cleaning materials for factory machinery	315				
Sundry factory expenses	872				
Salaries of office staff	6,545				
Repairs to sales staff cars	731				
Depreciation of office equipment	200				
Magazine advertising	1,508				
Sundry office expenses	403				
Hire of display stands used at garden centres	500				
Office stationery	276				
TOTALS	47,005				

2 Chapter activities
Materials costs

2.1 You have the following information for boxes of 500 C5 envelopes:

- annual usage   200 boxes
- ordering cost   £30.00 per order
- inventory holding cost   £1.20 per box per year

What is the Economic Order Quantity (EOQ)?

	✔
25 boxes	
50 boxes	
100 boxes	
200 boxes	

2.2 The supplies department of Peoples Bank has the following movements of an item of inventory for June 20-3:

		units	cost per unit £	total cost £
1 June	Balance	2,000	2.00	4,000
15 June	Receipts	1,500	2.35	3,525
21 June	Issues	3,000		

You are to complete the following table for FIFO and AVCO:

DATE 20-3	DESCRIPTION	FIFO £	AVCO £
21 June	Total issue value		
30 June	Total closing inventory value		

2.3 Wyezed Limited manufactures a product using two types of materials, Wye and Zed. The accounting policy of the company is to issue material Wye to production using the FIFO method, and material Zed on the AVCO method.

The following are the inventory movements of materials during the month of August 20-1:

Material Wye – FIFO method

		kilos (kg)	cost per kg
20-1			£
1 Aug	Balance	5,000	5.00
10 Aug	Receipts	2,000	5.25
18 Aug	Receipts	3,000	5.50
23 Aug	Issues	8,000	

Material Zed – AVCO method

		kilos (kg)	cost per kg
20-1			£
1 Aug	Balance	10,000	4.00
6 Aug	Receipts	5,000	4.30
19 Aug	Receipts	6,000	4.45
24 Aug	Issues	12,000	

(a) You are to complete the inventory records, on the next page, for material Wye and material Zed.

INVENTORY RECORD: FIFO

Product: Material Wye

Date	Receipts			Issues			Balance		
20-1	Quantity (kgs)	Cost per kg	Total Cost	Quantity (kgs)	Cost per kg	Total Cost	Quantity (kgs)	Cost per kg	Total Cost
1 Aug	Balance	£	£		£	£	5,000	£ 5.00	£ 25,000
10 Aug	2,000	5.25	10,500						
18 Aug	3,000	5.50	16,500						
23 Aug									

INVENTORY RECORD: AVCO

Product: Material Zed

Date	Receipts			Issues			Balance		
20-1	Quantity (kgs)	Cost per kg	Total Cost	Quantity (kgs)	Cost per kg	Total Cost	Quantity (kgs)	Cost per kg	Total Cost
1 Aug	Balance	£	£		£	£	10,000	£ 4.00	£ 40,000
6 Aug	5,000	4.30	21,500						
19 Aug	6,000	4.45	26,700						
24 Aug									

(b)   At 31 August 20-1, the net realisable value of each type of inventory is:

- material Wye   £10,000
- material Zed   £44,000

Fill in the box with the amount at which inventories should be valued on 31 August 20-1 in order to comply with International Accounting Standard No 2 *Inventories*.

£

2.4 Wyevale Tutorial College is a private college which runs courses for local companies on business and management subjects. The inventory records of photocopying paper are maintained on the FIFO method at present. The College's accountant has suggested that a change should be made to the AVCO method.

As an accounts assistant you have been asked to prepare information based on the movements of photocopying paper for February 20-8 which are as follows:

1 February	Opening inventory	100 reams* at £2.00 per ream
5 February	Issues	50 reams
10 February	Purchases	150 reams at £2.20 per ream
15 February	Issues	100 reams
18 February	Purchases	200 reams at £2.30 per ream
24 February	Issues	120 reams
		* a ream is 500 sheets

You are to:

(a)   Complete the inventory record on the next page for February, using the FIFO method.

(b)   Complete the inventory record on page 15 for February, using the AVCO method.

(a)

INVENTORY RECORD: FIFO									
Product: Photocopying paper (reams)									
Date	Receipts			Issues			Balance		
20-8	Quantity (reams)	Cost per ream £	Total Cost £	Quantity (reams)	Cost per ream £	Total Cost £	Quantity (reams)	Cost per ream £	Total Cost £
1 Feb	Balance						100	2.00	200

(b)

INVENTORY RECORD: AVCO								
Product: Photocopying paper (reams)								
Date	**Receipts**			**Issues**			**Balance**		
20-8	Quantity (reams)	Cost per ream £	Total Cost £	Quantity (reams)	Cost per ream £	Total Cost £	Quantity (reams)	Cost per ream £	Total Cost £
1 Feb	Balance						100	2.00	200

2.5 A football club shop sells replica club strips, as well as other goods and clothing. The club strip has recently been changed and the old version will have to be sold at greatly reduced prices. At the end of the financial year, the inventories in the shop include:

	Cost	Net realisable value
	£	£
Replica strip (old version)	3,800	2,500
Replica strip (new version)	8,400	11,000
	12,200	13,500

What is the total value of the inventory items above, which complies with International Accounting Standard No 2 *Inventories*?

	✔
£12,200	
£13,500	
£10,900	
£14,800	

2.6 SummerDaze Limited manufactures plastic garden furniture. Its best seller is the 'Calypso' seat made from white plastic.

The company uses the first in, first out (FIFO) method of issuing inventories.

As an accounts assistant at SummerDaze you have been given the following tasks.

Task 1

Complete the following inventory record for white plastic for April 20-9:

INVENTORY RECORD: FIFO

Product: White plastic

Date	Receipts			Issues			Balance	
	Quantity (kgs)	Cost per kg	Total Cost	Quantity (kgs)	Cost per kg	Total Cost	Quantity (kgs)	Total Cost
20-9		£	£		£	£		£
Balance at 1 April							20,000	20,000
7 April	10,000	1.10	11,000				30,000	31,000
12 April				25,000				
20 April	20,000	1.20	24,000					
23 April				15,000				

Task 2

All issues of white plastic are for the manufacture of the 'Calypso' seat. The following cost accounting codes are used to record materials costs:

code number	description
2000	inventory – white plastic
2100	production – Calypso seats
3000	trade payables/purchases ledger control

Complete the following table to record the journal entries for the two purchases and two issues of white plastic in the cost accounting records.

20-9	Code number	Debit £	Credit £
7 April			
7 April			
12 April			
12 April			
20 April			
20 April			
23 April			
23 April			

2.7 The following information is available for metal grade X8:

- Annual demand – 36,125 kilograms
- Annual holding cost per kilogram – £3
- Fixed ordering cost – £30

(a) You are to calculate the Economic Order Quantity (EOQ) for X8.

> EOQ = ...kg

The inventory record shown below for plastic grade X8 for the month of May has only been fully completed for the first three weeks of the month.

(b) Complete the entries in the inventory record for the two receipts on 24 and 27 May that were ordered using the EOQ method.

(c) Complete ALL entries in the inventory record for the two issues in the month and for the closing balance at the end of May using the AVCO method of issuing inventory.

Show the costs per kilogram (kg) in £ to 3 decimal places, and the total costs in whole £.

Inventory record for metal grade X8

Date	Receipts			Issues			Balance	
	Quantity (kg)	Cost per kg	Total Cost	Quantity (kg)	Cost per kg	Total Cost	Quantity (kg)	Total Cost
		£	£		£	£		£
Balance as at 22 May							420	1,512
24 May		3.711						
26 May				900				
27 May		3.755						
30 May				800				

2.8 Harvie Limited uses the following accounts to record inventory transactions in its cost book-keeping system:

– inventory account

– trade payables/purchases ledger control account

– bank account

– production account

For each of the five transactions in the following table show the account which will be debited and the account which will be credited.

	Transaction	Account debited	Account credited
1.	Receipt of materials into inventory, paying immediately by BACS		
2.	Issue of materials from inventory to production		
3.	Receipt of materials into inventory, purchased from a credit supplier		
4.	Return of poor quality materials to a credit supplier		
5.	Return of surplus materials from production to inventory		

2.9   Indicate the statements which apply to the method(s) of inventory valuation. Note: statements may apply to more than one method.

Statement	FIFO ✔	LIFO ✔	AVCO ✔
issues from inventory are from the most recent receipts			
in times of rising prices, reported profits will usually be lower than with other methods			
closing inventory is based on more recent costs of goods received			
issues from inventory are from the earliest receipts			
acceptable for tax purposes			
closing inventory is valued at a weighted average cost			
permitted by IAS 2, *Inventories*			
in times of rising prices the cost of sales figure will usually be lower than with other methods			
closing inventory is based on older costs of goods received			

3 Chapter activities
Labour costs

3.1 Renne Limited pays its employees their basic pay at a time rate per hour, for a 35-hour week.

For any overtime in excess of 35 hours per week, the extra hours are paid at basic pay plus an overtime premium. There are two overtime premium rates:

- rate 1 for weekdays, with an overtime premium equal to one-third of basic pay

- rate 2 for weekends, with an overtime premium equal to half of basic pay

The details of three employees for last week are as follows:

Employee	Time rate per hour	Total hours worked	Overtime rate 1 (hours)	Overtime rate 2 (hours)
L Constantinou	£12.80	40	–	5
H Gunther	£15.00	38	2	1
J White	£10.20	42	5	2

Complete the table below to show the basic pay, overtime premium, and gross pay for the week.

Employee	Basic pay £	Overtime premium rate 1 £	Overtime premium rate 2 £	Gross pay for week £
L Constantinou				
H Gunther				
J White				

3.2 Elend Limited, a manufacturing company, pays its production-line employees on a piecework basis, but with a guaranteed time rate for the hours worked. The details of three employees for last week are as follows:

Employee	Time rate per hour	Hours worked	Production for week	Piecework rate
J Daniels	£12.00	38	800 units	55p per unit
L Ho	£11.50	35	650 units	65p per unit
T Turner	£11.75	36	500 units	90p per unit

Complete the table below to show the time rate, piecework rate, and the gross pay for the week.

Employee	Time rate £	Piecework rate £	Gross pay for week £
J Daniels			
L Ho			
T Turner			

3.3 Brock and Company, a manufacturing business, pays its production-line employees on a time basis. A bonus is paid where production is completed faster than the time allowed. The bonus is 50 per cent of the time saved and is paid at the time rate per hour. The details of four employees for last week are as follows:

Employee	Time rate per hour	Hours worked	Allowed per hour	Actual production
H Hands	£12.50	35	50 units	1,950 units
A Khan	£11.75	37	60 units	2,200 units
T Shah	£11.00	38	50 units	2,000 units
D Smith	£12.80	40	60 units	2,490 units

Note: there were no overtime payments last week.

Complete the table below to show the time rate, bonus (if any), and gross pay for the week.

Employee	Time rate £	Bonus £	Gross pay for week £
H Hands			
A Khan			
T Shah			
D Smith			

3.4 SummerDaze Limited manufactures plastic garden furniture. Its best seller is the 'Calypso' seat made from white plastic.

The payroll for the week ended 18 June 20-9 has been completed, with the following amounts to pay:

		£
•	net wages to be paid to employees	8,000
•	income tax and National Insurance Contributions (NIC) to be paid to HM Revenue and Customs	1,650
•	pension contributions to be paid to the pension fund	850
	PAYROLL FOR THE WEEK	10,500

The payroll for the week has been analysed as:

		£
•	direct labour costs	7,750
•	indirect labour costs	1,500
•	administration labour costs	1,250
		10,500

As an accounts assistant at SummerDaze you have been given the following tasks:

Task 1

Prepare wages control account for the week ended 18 June 20-9:

Dr		**Wages Control Account**		Cr
	£			£

Task 2

All of the direct labour costs are for the manufacture of 'Calypso' seats. The following cost accounting codes are in use to record labour costs:

code number	description
2100	production – Calypso seats
2200	production overheads
2300	non-production overheads – administration
3100	wages control

Complete the table below to record the journal entries which show how the total cost of the payroll is split between the various cost centres of the business.

20-9	Code number	Debit £	Credit £
18 June	2100		
18 June	3100		
18 June	2200		
18 June	3100		
18 June	2300		
18 June	3100		

3.5   Perran Limited manufactures surf boards. The following data relates to the production of its 'Porth' brand of board for February 20-6:

Total direct labour hours worked	3,000 hours
Normal time hours	2,600 hours
Overtime hours	400 hours
Normal time rate per hour	£10 per hour
Overtime premium per hour	£5 per hour

In the company's cost book-keeping system all direct labour overtime payments are included in direct costs.

The following cost accounting codes are in use to record labour costs:

code number	description
2100	production – 'Porth' boards
4400	wages control

(a)   Calculate the total cost of direct labour for February

Total cost of direct labour for February:

(b)   State the cost book-keeping entries, together with account codes, which will transfer the direct labour costs to production

Account name	Account code	Debit £	Account name	Account code	Credit £

3.6 You are an accounts assistant at Cooper Limited and have been asked to help with calculating labour costs.

The cost accountant has given you the following time sheet for one of Cooper Limited's employees, S Patton, who is paid as follows:

- For a basic six-hour shift every day from Monday to Friday – basic pay

- For any overtime in excess of the basic six hours on any day from Monday to Friday – the extra hours are paid at time-and-a-half (basic pay plus an overtime premium equal to half of basic pay)

- For three contracted hours each Saturday morning – basic pay

- For any hours worked in excess of three hours on a Saturday or any hours worked on a Sunday – double-time (basic pay plus an overtime premium equal to basic pay)

You are to complete the time sheet columns headed basic pay, overtime premium and total pay (enter a zero figure, '0', in the columns where nothing is to be paid).

Employee's weekly time sheet for week ending 11 August 20-8

Employee: S Patton			Profit Centre: Moulding			
Employee number: 617			Basic pay per hour: £12.00			
	Hours spent on production	Hours worked on indirect work	Notes	Basic pay £	Overtime premium £	Total pay £
Monday	6	0				
Tuesday	7	0				
Wednesday	6	2	10 am-12 noon training			
Thursday	8	0				
Friday	6	1	8 am-9 am maintenance			
Saturday	4	0				
Sunday	2	0				
Total	39	3				

3.7   Indicate the statements which apply to the method(s) of labour costs. Note: statements may apply to more than one method.

Statement	Time rate ✔	Piecework rate ✔	Bonus system ✔
The gross pay calculation is: hours worked x rate per hour			
Method used for repetitive work where output is more important than quality			
The gross pay calculation is: gross pay + proportion of the time saved			
The employer has to set time allowances for work done			
Pay is not linked to output			
Employees can earn more by working harder			
There is no pressure on time, so quality of output should be maintained			
The amount earned by employees varies with output			
The gross pay calculation is: number of items produced x rate per item			

4

Chapter activities
Expenses

4.1 Classify the following costs:

	capital expenditure ✔	revenue expenditure ✔
(a) building an extension to the administration office		
(b) cleaning materials for factory machinery		
(c) repair of office photocopier		
(d) directors' salaries		
(e) carriage inwards on new machinery		
(f) carriage inwards on raw materials		
(g) installation of computer system		
(h) insurance of computer system		
(i) installation of special wiring for computer system		

4.2   Classify the following costs:

	DIRECT EXPENSES ✔	INDIRECT EXPENSES	
		production overheads ✔	non-production overheads ✔
(a) royalties paid to designer of product			
(b) straight-line depreciation of factory machinery			
(c) office electricity			
(d) insurance of factory buildings			
(e) advertising			
(f) rent on factory			
(g) units of output depreciation of factory machinery			
(h) factory manager's car expenses			
(i) sales department administration			

4.3   Greenacres Limited manufactures two types of garden lawnmower – the 'Alpha', an electric mower, and the 'Beta', a petrol mower. The general expenses account for the month ended 30 November 20-4 has a debit balance of £34,500. This balance is analysed as:

		£
•	direct expenses – Alpha	8,390
•	direct expenses – Beta	6,240
•	production overheads	13,850
•	non-production overheads – selling and distribution	3,170
•	non-production overheads – administration	2,850
		34,500

The following cost accounting codes are in use to record expenses:

code number	description
1500	production – Alpha
1600	production – Beta
2000	production overheads
2500	non-production overheads – selling and distribution
2600	non-production overheads – administration
3000	general expenses

As an accounts assistant at Greenacres Limited you have been given the following tasks:

Task 1
Prepare general expenses account for the month ended 30 November 20-4:

Dr			**General Expenses Account (3000)**		Cr
20-4		£	20-4		£
30 Nov	Balance b/d	34,500			

Task 2

Complete the following table below to record the journal entries which show how the total cost of general expenses is split between production, prcduction overheads and non-production overheads.

20-4	Code number	Debit £	Credit £
30 Nov	1500		
30 Nov	3000		
30 Nov	1600		
30 Nov	3000		
30 Nov	2000		
30 Nov	3000		
30 Nov	2500		
30 Nov	3000		
30 Nov	2600		
30 Nov	3000		

4.4 In the graphs below, draw in the lines to show how fixed costs and variable costs behave with changes in the level of activity.

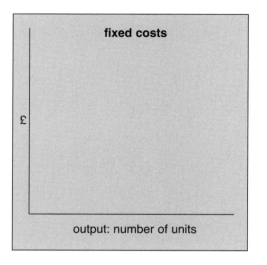

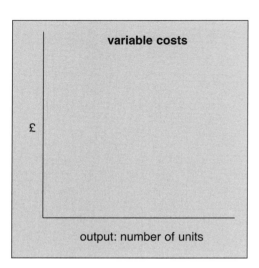

4.5   Classify the following costs:

	fixed ✔	semi-variable ✔	variable ✔
(a) rent of business premises			
(b) week's hire of machinery at £100 per week for one particular job			
(c) telephone system with a fixed line rental and a cost per call			
(d) supervisor's wages			
(e) reducing balance depreciation			
(f) production-line employees paid a basic wage, with a bonus linked to output			
(g) royalty paid to author for each book sold			
(h) accountant's fees			
(i) raw materials used in production			

4.6 The accounts supervisor of Darnbrook Limited provides you with the following information:

- at 20,000 units of output, total costs are £350,000
- at 30,000 units of output, total costs are £500,000

You are to use the high/low method to identify the amount of fixed costs. The supervisor tells you that there is a constant unit variable cost up to this volume, and that there are no stepped fixed costs.

Fill in the following with your answer:

Fixed costs, at these levels of output are	£

4.7   Khan Manufacturing has forecast its revenue and costs for 20-2 on the basis of sales and output of 12,000 units as follows:

		£
sales revenue		144,000
variable costs	– materials	36,000
	– labour	24,000
	– expenses	6,000
fixed costs	– labour	18,500
	– overheads	25,250

The sales department thinks that demand for the product is more likely to be 15,000 units, or could be as high as 20,000 units.

You are to complete the table below and calculate the estimated cost per unit and profit per unit at the different activity levels. (Note: you may assume that there is a constant unit variable cost up to this volume, and that there are no stepped fixed costs.)

20-2 FORECAST REVENUE AND COSTS			
UNITS PRODUCED AND SOLD	12,000	15,000	20,000
	£	£	£
Sales revenue			
Variable costs			
Materials			
Labour			
Expenses			
Fixed costs			
Labour			
Overheads			
Total costs			
Total profit			
Cost per unit (to 2 decimal places)			
Profit per unit (to 2 decimal places)			

4.8   Croome Limited makes controllers for hot water systems – both domestic and commercial use. The company has prepared a forecast for the next quarter for one of its controllers, CC8. This controller is produced in batches and the forecast is based on selling and producing 1,000 batches.

One of the customers of Croome Limited has indicated that it may be significantly increasing its order level for controller CC8 for the next quarter and it appears that activity levels of 1,500 batches and 1,800 batches are feasible.

The semi-variable costs should be calculated using the high/low method. If 3,000 batches are sold the total semi-variable cost will be £8,000 and there is a constant unit variable cost up to this volume.

Complete the table below and calculate the estimated profit per batch of CC8 at the different activity levels.

Batches produced and sold	1,000	1,500	1,800
	£	£	£
Sales revenue	45,000	67,500	81,000
Variable costs:			
• Direct materials	10,000	15,000	18,000
• Direct labour	12,000	18,000	21,600
• Overheads	8,000	12,000	14,400
Semi-variable costs:	4,000	5,000	5,600
• Variable element	2,000	3,000	3,600
• Fixed element	2,000	2,000	2,000
Total cost	34,000	50,000	59,600
Total profit	11,000	17,500	21,400
Profit per batch (to 2 decimal places)	11.00	11.67	11.89

5 Chapter activities
Overheads

5.1 Mereford Management College is a private college that has two teaching departments – accountancy and management.

The College charges overheads on the basis of teaching hours. The overhead analysis information which follows is available to you.

OVERHEAD ANALYSIS January 20-7		
	Accountancy Department	Management Department
Budgeted total overheads (£)	15,884	19,855
Budgeted teaching hours	722	1,045
Budgeted overhead absorption rate (£)		

You are to calculate the budgeted overhead absorption rate for each of the two departments.

Details of a particular course – 'Finance for Managers' – that is taught in both the accountancy and management departments are as follows.

OVERHEAD ANALYSIS Course: Finance for Managers		
	Accountancy Department	Management Department
Teaching hours	45	20
Budgeted overhead absorption rate (£)		
Overhead absorbed by course (£)		

You are to calculate the overhead absorbed by the 'Finance for Managers' course.

5.2 Wyevale Processing Limited processes and packs fruit and vegetables for supermarkets. The company has five departments – processing, packing, quality assurance, stores and maintenance.

The accounts supervisor has given you the budgeted production overhead schedule (see next page) to complete for next month.

The following information is available:

	Processing	Packing	Quality Assurance	Stores	Maintenance
Floor area (square metres)	160	210	50	80	100
Employees (number)	10	14	2	2	2
Equipment usage (hours)	300	100	40		

You are to complete the budgeted production overhead schedule for next month showing the basis of apportionment to the five departments of the business.

WYEVALE PROCESSING LIMITED

BUDGETED PRODUCTION OVERHEAD SCHEDULE

for next month

Budgeted overhead	Basis of apportionment	Totals £	Processing £	Packing £	Quality Assurance £	Stores £	Maintenance £
Rent and rates		4,500					
Supervisors' salaries		3,690					
Depreciation of equipment		2,640					
Canteen costs		720					
TOTAL		11,550					

5.3 Wyvern Private Hospital plc has two patient wards – a day care ward for minor operations where the patients go home at the end of the day, and a surgical ward for patients who remain in the hospital for several days. There are two service departments – the operating theatre and administration.

The overheads of each department for last month were as follows:

		£
•	day care ward	28,750
•	surgical ward	42,110
•	operating theatre	32,260
•	administration	9,075

The basis for re-apportioning the overheads of the service departments is:

- operating theatre, on the number of operations carried out – day care ward, 160; surgical ward, 120

- administration, on the number of staff in each department – day care ward, 10; surgical ward, 25; operating theatre, 20

You are to complete the table below, using the step-down method, to re-apportion the two service department overheads to the two patient wards.

	Day care ward £	Surgical ward £	Operating theatre £	Administration £	Totals £
Overheads					
Reapportion Administration					
Reapportion Operating theatre					
Total overheads to patient wards					

5.4 Milestone Motors Limited sells and services cars. The company's operations are organised into three profit centres and one cost centre, as follows:

Profit centres
- New car sales
- Used car sales
- Servicing

Cost centre
- Administration

The budgeted overheads of the company for the four weeks ended 28 April 20-2 are:

	£
Depreciation of non-current assets	8,400
Rent	10,000
Other property overheads	4,500
Staff costs:	
− new car sales	11,080
− used car sales	7,390
− servicing	9,975
− administration	6,850
Administration overheads	3,860
Total	62,055

The following information is also relevant:

Profit/Cost centre	% of floor space occupied	Carrying amount of non-current assets £000
New car sales	40%	50
Used car sales	30%	30
Servicing	20%	100
Administration	10%	20
	100%	200

Overheads are allocated and apportioned using the most appropriate basis. The total administration overheads are then re-apportioned to the three profit centres using the following percentages.
- New car sales   20%
- Used car sales   30%
- Servicing   50%

Task 1

Complete the following table showing:

• the basis for allocation or apportionment of each overhead;

• the allocation and apportionment of fixed overheads between the four centres;

• the re-apportionment of the total administration overheads.

Budgeted overheads for four weeks ended 28 April 20-2	Basis of apportion- ment	Totals £	New Car Sales £	Used Car Sales £	Servicing £	Administration £
Depreciation of non-current assets		8,400				
Rent		10,000				
Other property overheads		4,500				
Staff costs		35,295				
Administration overheads		3,860				
		62,055				( )
Administration		62,055				–

Task 2

Servicing centre overheads are absorbed on the basis of budgeted direct labour hours. The budgeted number of direct labour hours for the servicing centre during the four weeks ended 28 April 20-2 is 1,025 hours.

What is the budgeted overhead absorption rate per direct labour hour for the servicing centre during the period?

£	per direct labour hour

5.5 You work as an accounts assistant for Trujillo Limited, a manufacturing business. The company has two production cost centres: cutting and assembly – and three support cost centres: maintenance, stores and administration.

Trujillo Limited's budgeted overheads for the next financial year are:

	£	£
Depreciation of equipment		4,200
Power for production machinery		2,040
Rent and rates		6,500
Light and heat		2,750
Indirect labour costs:		
Maintenance	38,550	
Stores	29,850	
Administration	51,250	
Totals	119,650	15,490

The following information is also available:

Department	Carrying amount (net book value) of equipment	Production machinery power usage (KwH)	Floor space (square metres)	Number of employees
Production cost centres:				
Cutting	100,000	15,000		4
Assembly	40,000	2,000		6
Support cost centres:				
Maintenance			100	2
Stores			160	2
Administration			240	3
Total	140,000	17,000	500	17

Overheads are allocated or apportioned on the most appropriate basis. The total overheads of the support cost centres are then reapportioned to the two production centres, using the direct method.

- 75% of the maintenance cost centre's time is spent maintaining machinery in the cutting production centre and the remainder in the assembly production centre.

- The stores cost centre makes 60% of its issues to the cutting production centre, and 40% to the assembly production centre.

- Administration supports the two production centres equally.

- There is no reciprocal servicing between the three support cost centres.

You are to complete the apportionment table below using the data above.

	Basis of apportionment	Cutting £	Assembly £	Maintenance £	Stores £	Admin £	Totals £
Depreciation of equipment							
Power for production machinery							
Rent and rates							
Light and heat							
Indirect labour							
Totals							
Reapportion Maintenance							
Reapportion Stores							
Reapportion Administration							
Total overheads to production centres							

5.6   Blenheim Limited's budgeted overheads and activity levels for the next quarter are:

	Moulding	Finishing
Budgeted overheads (£)	39,600	62,700
Budgeted direct labour hours	2,475	4,180
Budgeted machine hours	4,400	2,850

1.   **What would be the budgeted overhead absorption rate for each department if this were set based on their both being heavily automated?**

	✔
moulding £9 per hour; finishing £15 per hour	
moulding £16 per hour; finishing £22 per hour	
moulding £9 per hour; finishing £22 per hour	
moulding £16 per hour; finishing £15 per hour	

2.   **What would be the budgeted overhead absorption rate for each department if this were set based on their both being labour intensive?**

	✔
moulding £9 per hour; finishing £15 per hour	
moulding £16 per hour; finishing £22 per hour	
moulding £9 per hour; finishing £22 per hour	
moulding £16 per hour; finishing £15 per hour	

Additional data

At the end of the quarter actual overheads incurred were found to be:

	Moulding	Finishing
Actual overheads (£)	41,200	61,800

3.   **Assuming that exactly the same amount of overheads was absorbed as budgeted, what were the budgeted under or over absorptions in the quarter?**

	✔
moulding over absorbed £1,600; finishing over absorbed £900	
moulding over absorbed £1,600; finishing under absorbed £900	
moulding under absorbed £1,600; finishing under absorbed £900	
moulding under absorbed £1,600; finishing over absorbed £900	

5.7   Garden Cottage Limited manufactures 'homestyle' soups which are sold through supermarkets and convenience stores. The soups pass through two departments – kitchen and canning. Details of overheads for the departments for the four weeks ended 16 June 20-6 are as follows:

Kitchen Department

- overhead absorption rate is £7.00 per direct labour hour
- direct labour hours worked were 800
- actual cost of production overhead was £5,000

Canning Department

- overhead absorption rate is £8.00 per machine hour
- machine hours worked were 400
- actual cost of production overhead was £3,500

The following cost accounting codes are in use to record overheads:

code number	description
2000	production
2100	production overheads: kitchen department
2200	production overheads: canning department
4000	income statement

As an accounts assistant at Garden Cottage Limited, you are asked to prepare the two production overheads accounts below and to fill in the table as at 16 June 20-6 to account for the overheads and the over and under absorption of overheads.

Dr	**Production Overheads Account: Kitchen Department**	Cr
£		£

Dr	**Production Overheads Account: Canning Department**	Cr
£		£

20-6	Code number	Debit £	Credit £

6 Chapter activities
Methods of costing

6.1 OB Printers has been asked by John Dun, a local poet, to quote for the cost of printing a small book of poetry. John Dun is not sure how many copies to order, and has asked for quotations for 500, 1,000 and 2,000 copies.

The estimates by OB Printers are as follows:

Setting up the printing machine:	6 hours at £10.00 per hour
Artwork:	7 hours at £12.00 per hour
Page setting:	20 hours at £15.00 per hour
Paper (for 500 copies):	£200.00
Other printing consumables (for 500 copies):	£100.00
Direct labour (for 500 copies):	5 hours at £13.00 per hour
Production overheads:	80% of direct labour costs
Profit:	25% of cost price

Task 1

Complete the Job Cost Sheet (see next page) for 500, 1,000 and 2,000 copies to show the estimated total cost of the job, and the selling price.

Task 2

Calculate the cost per book (to the nearest penny) to the author at each of the three different production levels.

	Cost per book to author:
500 copies	£
1,000 copies	£
2,000 copies	£

JOB NO 12345

Poetry book for John Dun

	NUMBER OF COPIES		
	500	**1,000**	**2,000**
	£	£	£
Fixed Costs			
Setting up machine			
Artwork			
Page setting			
Direct Materials			
Paper			
Other printing consumables			
Direct Labour			
Production Overheads			
TOTAL COST			
Profit (25% of total cost)			
SELLING PRICE			

6.2 A manufacturer of security alarms has the following information concerning the first month of production:

Direct materials	£10,725
Direct labour	£6,600
Production overheads	£3,900
Security alarms completed	2,750
Security alarms in progress	500

The work-in-progress is complete as regards materials, but is 50% complete as regards direct labour and production overheads.

You are to complete the following layout to show the cost per security alarm of the first month's production and the month-end valuation for work-in-progress.

Cost element	Costs	Completed Units	Work-in-progress			Total Equivalent Units	Cost per Unit	WIP valuation
			Units	% complete	Equivalent Units			
	A	B	C	D	E	F	G	H
					C x D	B + E	A ÷ F	E x G
	£						£	£
Direct materials								
Direct labour								
Production overheads								
Total								

6.3   Wyvern Chemicals Limited produces a chemical, which is made in one production process.

For the four weeks ended 9 April 20-4, the company input 65,000 litres of direct materials, had an output of 60,000 litres and a normal loss of 5,000 litres. The input costs were: materials £19,500, labour £13,000, overheads £9,750. Normal losses were sold to a specialist reprocessing company for 5p per litre.

There was no opening or closing inventory at the beginning and end of the process; all output was complete.

As an accounts assistant, you are to complete the following process account and the normal loss account for the four weeks ended 9 April 20-4.

Dr				**Process Account**				Cr
	Quantity	Unit cost	Total cost		Quantity	Unit cost	Total cost
	(litres)	£	£		(litres)	£	£
Materials				Normal loss			
Labour				Finished goods			
Overheads							

Dr	**Normal Loss Account**		Cr
	£		£

6.4 Hawke Limited produces a washing powder called 'CleanO', which is made in one production process.

For the four weeks ended 24 September 20-3, the company input 84,000 kilos of direct materials, had an output of 81,000 kilos – the difference of 3,000 kilos was made up of a normal loss of 4,000 kilos and an abnormal gain of 1,000 kilos.

The input costs were: materials £16,800, labour £12,600, overheads £4,200. All losses were sold to a specialist reprocessing company for 20p per kilo.

There was no opening or closing inventory at the beginning and end of the process; all output was complete.

As an accounts assistant, you are to complete the following process account, the abnormal gain account, and the normal loss account for the four weeks ended 24 September 20-3.

Dr				Process Account				Cr
	Quantity	Unit cost	Total cost			Quantity	Unit cost	Total cost
	(kilos)	£	£			(kilos)	£	£
Materials				Normal loss				
Labour				Finished goods				
Overheads								
Abnormal gain								

Dr	Normal Loss Account	Cr
	£	£

Dr	Abnormal Gain Account	Cr
	£	£

6.5 Burncoose Limited is a manufacturer of vitamin tablets. Its best-selling product, called 'Vita' is made in two production processes before completion and transfer to finished goods.

For the four weeks ended 16 July 20-4, details of production of 'Vita' were as follows:

	Process 1	Process 2
Direct materials (5,000 kilos)	£2,000	–
Labour	£1,000	£1,125
Overheads	£500	£675
Normal loss in process	5% of input	3% of input
Output	4,500 kilos	4,400 kilos
Scrap value of all losses	£0.20 per kilo	£0.40 per kilo

There was no opening or closing inventory at the beginning and end of either process; all output was complete. All losses were sold to a specialist reprocessing company.

As an accounts assistant, you are to complete the following process 1 account, process 2 account, normal loss account, abnormal loss account and abnormal gain account for the four weeks ended 16 July 20-4. Note: show cost per unit of expected output to the nearest penny.

Dr				Process 1 Account				Cr
	Quantity	Unit cost	Total cost		Quantity	Unit cost	Total cost	
	(kilos)	£	£		(kilos)	£	£	
Materials				Normal loss				
Labour				Transfer to				
Overheads				process 2				
				Abnormal loss				

Dr				Process 2 Account				Cr
	Quantity	Unit cost	Total cost		Quantity	Unit cost	Total cost	
	(kilos)	£	£		(kilos)	£	£	
Transfer from				Normal loss				
process 1				Finished goods				
Labour								
Overheads								
Abnormal gain								

Dr		**Normal Loss Account**		Cr
	£			£

Dr		**Abnormal Loss Account**		Cr
	£			£

Dr		**Abnormal Gain Account**		Cr
	£			£

6.6 Zelah Chemicals Limited uses process costing for its products.

The process account for July for one particular process has been partly completed but the following information is also relevant:

- Four employees worked on this process during July. Each employee worked 35 hours per week for 4 weeks and was paid £12 per hour.

- Overheads are absorbed on the basis of £10 per labour hour.

- Zelah Chemicals Limited expects a normal loss of 5% during this process, which it then sells for scrap at 50p per kilo.

(a) Complete the process account below for July.

Description	kilos	Unit cost £	Total cost £	Description	kilos	Unit cost £	Total cost £
Material ZC6	300	1.60		Normal loss		0.50	
Material ZC8	1,500	0.80		Output	1,900		
Material ZC10	200	1.50					
Labour							
Overheads							

(b) Identify the correct entry for each of the following in a normal loss account.

	Debit ✓	Credit ✓
Process		
Abnormal gain		

7 Chapter activities
Marginal and absorption costing

7.1 Outdoor Limited makes garden seats. The management of the company is considering the production for next year and has asked for help with certain financial decisons.

The following information is available:

Selling price (per seat) £100

Direct materials (per seat) £25

Direct labour (per seat) £30

Fixed production overheads £100,000 per year

The company is planning to manufacture 4,000 seats next year.

REQUIRED

You are to calculate:

- the marginal cost per seat

- the absorption cost per seat

- the profit or loss if 4,000 seats are sold

Complete the table below with your answers:

Marginal cost per seat	£
Absorption cost per seat	£
Profit or loss if 4,000 seats are sold	£

7.2 Strellis Limited manufactures one product, the Strell. For the month of June 20-5 the following information is available:

Number of units manufactured	4,000
Number of units sold	3,500
Selling price	£10 per unit
Direct materials for month	£10,000
Direct labour for month	£12,000
Fixed production overheads for month	£15,000

There was no finished goods inventory at the start of the month. Both direct materials and direct labour are variable costs.

REQUIRED

(a)   produce income statements for June 20-5, using:

- marginal costing

- absorption costing

(b)   explain briefly the reason for the difference between recorded profits under the alternative costing methods

7.3 For a manufacturing business, which type of inventory is included in the calculation of prime cost?

	✔
direct materials	
work-in-progress	
partly manufactured goods	
finished goods	

7.4 In a manufacturing account, direct materials and direct labour are included in the calculation of:

	✔
prime cost	
production overheads	
non-production overheads	
indirect expenses	

7.5 Allocate the following costs to either the manufacturing account or the income statement by ticking the appropriate column in the table below:

	Manufacturing account ✔	Income statement ✔
salaries of sales staff		
wages of production-line employees		
royalty paid to designer of product		
straight-line depreciation of factory machinery		
factory power costs		
re-decoration of administration office		
interest on bank loan		

7.6   The following figures relate to the accounts of Middleton Manufacturing Company for the year
ended 31 December 20-5:

	£
Inventories at 1 January 20-5:	
Direct materials	25,250
Finished goods	12,380
Inventories at 31 December 20-5:	
Direct materials	29,610
Finished goods	11,490
Expenditure during year:	
Purchases of direct materials	75,340
Factory wages – direct	54,690
Factory wages – indirect	22,330
Factory rent and rates	7,380
Factory power	4,250
Depreciation of factory machinery	2,500
Repairs to factory buildings	1,870
Sundry factory expenses	1,140
Non-production overheads	46,730
Sales revenue for the year	286,940

Note: Factory power is to be treated as a production overhead.

You are to prepare the year end:
*   manufacturing account
*   income statement

A layout for a manufacturing account and an income statement is included in the Appendix of
Costs and revenues tutorial, and is also available in the Resources section of
www.osbornebooks.co.uk

7.7 The following figures relate to the accounts of Rashleigh Manufacturing Limited for the year ended 30 June 20-7:

	£
Inventory of direct materials at 1 July 20-6	22,840
Inventory of direct materials at 30 June 20-7	25,290
Inventory of work-in-progress at 1 July 20-6	10,470
Inventory of work-in-progress at 30 June 20-7	9,630
Inventory of finished goods at 1 July 20-6	33,640
Inventory of finished goods at 30 June 20-7	32,790
Purchases of direct materials	127,330
Revenue for the year	525,460
Rent and rates	24,560
Factory wages – direct	86,520
Factory wages – indirect	53,210
Factory power	9,760
Factory heat and light	2,150
Factory sundry expenses and maintenance	4,720
Administration salaries	77,280
Advertising	27,430
Office expenses	8,310
Depreciation of factory plant and machinery	15,000
Depreciation of office equipment	5,000

Additional information:
* factory power is to be treated as a production overhead
* rent and rates are to be allocated 75% to manufacturing and 25% to administration

You are to prepare the year end:
* manufacturing account
* income statement

A layout for a manufacturing account and an income statement is included in the Appendix of *Costs and revenues tutorial*, and is also available in the Resources section of www.osbornebooks.co.uk

8 Chapter activities
Aspects of budgeting

8.1   The budget for direct materials is £6,300; the actual cost is £6,100. The budget for direct labour is £8,900; the actual cost is £9,250.

Which one of the following statements is correct?

	✔
direct materials variance £200 adverse; direct labour variance £350 adverse	
direct materials variance £200 favourable; direct labour variance £350 favourable	
direct materials variance £200 adverse; direct labour variance £350 favourable	
direct materials variance £200 favourable; direct labour variance £350 adverse	

8.2   A budget for 10,000 units of output shows a direct materials cost of £5,600 and a direct labour cost of £8,200. Actual output is 11,000 units.

Which one of the following gives the correct figures for the flexed budget?

	✔
direct materials £5,600; direct labour £8,200	
direct materials £5,600; direct labour £9,020	
direct materials £6,160; direct labour £9,020	
direct materials £6,160; direct labour £8,200	

8.3   Identify the correct variance from the causes of variances given by putting a tick in the relevant column of the table below.

Cause of variance	Adverse ✔	Favourable ✔
decrease in cost of direct materials		
more materials are wasted		
more expensive direct materials are used		
specifications are changed to use cheaper materials		
a cheaper grade of direct labour is employed		
machine speed is increased		
during the recession direct labour agrees to work an extra hour a week for no pay		
the cost of power for the machines increases		
a fluctuation in exchange rates increases the cost of imported raw materials		
selling prices are reduced		
there is a decrease in the volume of output sold		

8.4 You work as an accounts assistant for Chorlton Limited, a manufacturing business.

You have been given the original budget costs and the actual performance for last month for product CH05. Actual output was 95 per cent of budgeted output.

You are asked to complete the flexible budget report, below, including the actual performance and the variances for last month from the following information:

	budget £	actual £
Direct materials	3,600	3,500
Direct labour	9,400	9,350
Overheads	7,500	7,300

Both direct materials and direct labour are variable costs, but the overheads are fixed.

In the budget report indicate whether the variance is Favourable or Adverse by entering F or V in the final column; if neither F nor V, enter 0.

BUDGET REPORT				
	Flexed budget	**Actual**	**Variance**	**Favourable (F) or Adverse (A)**
Output level	95%			
	£	£	£	
Direct materials				
Direct labour				
Overheads				
TOTAL				

8.5 Melia Ltd has the following original budget and actual performance for product M55 for the year ending 31 December.

	budget	actual
Volume sold	50,000	45,000
	£000	£000
Sales revenue	1,200	1,050
Less costs:		
Direct materials	300	260
Direct labour	400	410
Overheads	350	330
Operating profit	150	50

Both direct materials and direct labour are variable costs, but the overheads are fixed.

You are to complete the following table to show a flexed budget and the resulting variances against this budget for the year. Show the actual variance amount, for sales and each cost, in the column headed 'Variance' and indicate whether this is Favourable or Adverse by entering F or A in the final column. If neither F nor A, enter 0.

	Flexed budget	Actual	Variance	Favourable (F) or Adverse (A)
Volume sold		45,000		
	£000	£000	£000	
Sales revenue		1,050		
Less costs:				
Direct materials		260		
Direct labour		410		
Overheads		330		
Operating profit		50		

8.6 Rehman Ltd has the following original budget and actual performance for product R10 for the year ending 31 December.

	budget	actual
Volume sold	6,000	6,450
	£000	£000
Sales revenue	840	910
Less costs:		
Direct materials	160	190
Direct labour	240	255
Overheads	280	300
Operating profit	160	165

Both direct materials and direct labour are variable costs, but the overheads are fixed.

You are to complete the following table to show a flexed budget and the resulting variances against this budget for the year. Show the actual variance amount, for sales and each cost, in the column headed 'Variance' and indicate whether this is Favourable or Adverse by entering F or A in the final column. If neither F nor A, enter 0.

	Flexed budget	**Actual**	**Variance**	**Favourable (F) or Adverse (A)**
Volume sold		6,450		
	£000	£000	£000	
Sales revenue		910		
Less costs:				
Direct materials		190		
Direct labour		255		
Overheads		300		
Operating profit		165		

9

Chapter activities
Short-term decisions

9.1   Bert Peters is the owner of a petrol filling station. He provides you with the following information:

cost of petrol from oil company	£1.20 per litre
selling price	£1.25 per litre
fixed costs for the week	£750

(a)   As an accounts assistant, you are to complete the following table showing his weekly costs, sales revenue and profit or loss:

units of output (litres)	fixed costs	variable costs	total cost	sales revenue	profit/(loss)
	£	£	£	£	£
0					
5,000					
10,000					
15,000					
16,000					
17,000					
18,000					
19,000					
20,000					

(b)   If sales are currently 18,000 litres each week, calculate the margin of safety, expressed in litres, as a percentage (to the nearest percentage point).

Margin of safety at sales of 18,000 litres	litres	%

9.2   Angrave Limited makes a product which is numbered AN02. The selling price of product AN02 is £22 per unit and the total variable cost is £14 per unit. Angrave Limited estimates that the fixed costs per quarter associated with this product are £12,000.

   (a)   **Calculate the budgeted breakeven, in units, for product AN02.**

units

   (b)   **Calculate the budgeted breakeven, in £, for product AN02.**

£

   (c)   **Complete the table below to show the budgeted margin of safety in units, and the margin of safety percentage if Angrave Limited sells 2,000 units or 2,500 units of product AN02.**

Units of AN02 sold	2,000	2,500
Margin of safety (units)		
Margin of safety (percentage)		

   (d)   **If Angrave Limited wishes to make a profit of £6,000, how many units of AN02 must it sell?**

units

   (e)   **If Angrave Limited increases the selling price of AN02 by £1, what will be the impact on the breakeven point and the margin of safety, assuming no change in the number of units sold?**

	✔
the breakeven point will decrease and the margin of safety will increase	
the breakeven point will stay the same but the margin of safety will decrease	
the breakeven point will decrease and the margin of safety will stay the same	
the breakeven point will increase and the margin of safety will decrease	

9.3 Nikko Limited has made the following estimates for next month:

Selling price	£20 per unit
Variable cost	£15 per unit
Fixed costs for the month	£100,000
Forecast output	25,000 units
Maximum output	35,000 units

As an accounts assistant, you are to carry out the following tasks:

Task 1

Calculate:

the contribution sales (CS) ratio	
the break-even point in units	
the break-even point in sales revenue	
the margin of safety in units at the forecast output	
the number of units to generate a profit of £50,000	

Task 2

Calculate the profit at:

the forecast output	
the maximum output	

9.4 Wyvern Porcelain Limited produces decorated porcelain figures which are sold in quality shops both in the UK and abroad.

There are three ranges of porcelain figures – 'people', 'animals' and 'birds'. The expected monthly costs and sales information for each range is as follows:

Product	'People'	'Animals'	'Birds'
Sales and production units*	1,000	2,000	2,700
Labour hours per month	1,500	1,000	900
Total sales revenue	£60,000	£55,000	£47,250
Total direct materials	£5,000	£6,000	£5,400
Total direct labour	£15,000	£10,000	£9,000
Total variable overheads	£10,000	£9,000	£8,000

* note: a unit is a porcelain figure

The total expected monthly fixed costs relating to the production of all porcelain figures are £45,400.

As an accounts assistant at Wyvern Porcelain Limited, you are to carry out the following tasks.

Task 1

Complete the table below to show for each product range the expected contribution per unit (to the nearest penny).

Product	'People'	'Animals'	'Birds'
Selling price per unit			
Less: Unit variable costs			
Direct materials			
Direct labour			
Variable overheads			
Contribution per unit			

Task 2

If the company only produces the 'People' range, calculate the number of units it would need to make and sell each month to cover the fixed costs of £45,400.

Break-even point for the 'People' range	units

Task 3

Making and painting the porcelain figures are highly skilled tasks, and unskilled labour cannot be brought in to cover for absent staff.

Because of staff holidays, the available labour hours for next month are reduced from 3,400 to 2,800. The finance director asks you to calculate the contribution of each unit (porcelain figure) per labour hour.

Using the data from Task 1, complete the table below (to two decimal places).

Product	'People'	'Animals'	'Birds'
Contribution per unit			
Labour hours per unit			
Contribution per labour hour			

Task 4

Using the data from Task 3, calculate how many units of each of product ranges 'People', 'Animals' and 'Birds' the company should make and sell in order to maximise its profits using 2,800 labour hours. Complete the table below to show the company's production plan for next month.

'People'	units
'Animals'	units
'Birds'	units

9.5 The Last Company is famous for its 'Snowdon' range of hill-walking boots. The management of the company is considering the production for next year and has asked for help with certain financial decisions.

The following information is available:

wholesale selling price (per pair)	£60
direct materials (per pair)	£20
direct labour (per pair)	£18
production overheads (fixed)	£200,000 per year

The company is planning to manufacture 12,500 pairs of boots next year.

You are to calculate:

- the absorption cost per pair

- the marginal cost per pair

- the profit or loss if 12,500 pairs of boots are sold

A mail order company, Sales-by-Post Limited, has approached The Last Company with a view to selling the 'Snowdon' boot through its catalogue. Sales-by-Post offers two contracts:

- either 2,500 pairs of boots at £45 per pair

- or 5,000 pairs of boots at £37 per pair

As The Last Company usually sells through specialist shops, it is not expected that 'normal' sales will be affected. These 'special orders' are within the capacity of the factory, and production overheads will remain unchanged.

As an accounts assistant, you are to advise the management whether these offers should be accepted; illustrate your answer with income statements.

10 Chapter activities
Long-term decisions

TABLE OF DISCOUNTED CASH FLOW FACTORS (to three decimal places)								
Cost of capital/ rate of return	10%	12%	14%	16%	18%	20%	22%	24%
Year 1	0.909	0.893	0.877	0.862	0.847	0.833	0.820	0.806
Year 2	0.826	0.797	0.769	0.743	0.718	0.694	0.672	0.650
Year 3	0.751	0.712	0.675	0.641	0.609	0.579	0.551	0.524
Year 4	0.683	0.636	0.592	0.552	0.516	0.482	0.451	0.423
Year 5	0.621	0.567	0.519	0.476	0.437	0.402	0.370	0.341
Year 6	0.564	0.507	0.456	0.410	0.370	0.335	0.303	0.275

Tutorial note: In Assessments you will always be given the appropriate factors.

10.1 The following information relates to two major capital investment projects being considered by Newell Limited. For financial reasons, only one project can be accepted.

	Project Ess	Project Tee
	£	£
Initial cost at the beginning of the project	100,000	115,000
Net cash inflows, year: 1	40,000	50,000
2	60,000	35,000
3	20,000	30,000
4	20,000	30,000
5	10,000	30,000
Expected scrap value at end of year 5	5,000	7,500

The initial cost occurs at the beginning of the project and you may assume that the net cash inflows will arise at the end of each year. Newell Limited requires an annual rate of return of 10 per cent.

To help the Managing Director of Newell Limited make her decision, as accounts assistant you are to:

- produce numerical assessments of the two projects based on the following capital investment appraisal methods:
  - (a)   the payback period
  - (b)   the net present value
- write a report to the Managing Director on the relative merits of the project appraisal methods, and advise her which capital investment, if either, should be undertaken

10.2 A capital investment project has the following expected cash flows over its life of three years:

		£
Initial cost at the beginning of the project		(55,000)
Net cash inflows, year:	1	19,376
	2	28,491
	3	21,053

The expected scrap value at the end of year 3 is nil.

You are to:

(a)   Calculate the net present value of the project at annual rates of return of 10 per cent, 12 per cent and 14 per cent. Calculate all money amounts to the nearest £.

(b)   What do your calculations in part (a) tell you about this project?

10.3 You work as an accounts assistant for the Chester Carpet Company, which makes quality carpets. Currently you are working on the appraisal of a capital investment project to purchase a new machine for the production department in December 20-1.

The machine will cost £65,000 and will have a useful life of four years. The cash inflows are expected to be:

	£
20-2	17,000
20-3	25,000
20-4	31,000
20-5	24,000

At the end of the project, the machine will be sold as scrap for an expected amount of £4,000.

Chester Carpet Company requires an annual rate of return of 10 per cent for net present value, and a maximum payback period of three years.

Task 1

Use the working paper on the next page to calculate the net present value and the payback period of the proposed project. Ignore inflation and calculate all money amounts to the nearest £.

Task 2

Write a report, dated 24 November 20-1, to the General Manager evaluating the proposal from a financial viewpoint. State any assumptions you have made in your analysis.

CHESTER CARPET LIMITED

Working paper for the financial appraisal of a new machine

for the production department

DISCOUNTED CASH FLOW

Year	Cash Flow	Discount Factor at 10%	Discounted Cash Flow
	£		£
20-1	_____	1.000	_____
20-2	_____	0.909	_____
20-3	_____	0.826	_____
20-4	_____	0.751	_____
20-5	_____	0.683	_____

Net Present Value (NPV)

PAYBACK PERIOD

Year	Cash Flow	Cumulative Cash Flow
	£	£
20-1	_____	_____
20-2	_____	_____
20-3	_____	_____
20-4	_____	_____
20-5	_____	_____

Payback period = _____

10.4 Towan Kitchens Limited makes 'flat-pack' kitchens which are sold to the public in DIY stores. You are an accounts assistant and have just received the following email from the General Manager:

EMAIL

From: General Manager

To: Accounts Assistant

Subject: Manufacture of kitchen worktops

Date: 15 September 20-4

As you know, the manufacture of worktops is currently contracted out to another company at a cost to us of £200,000 per year. The production manager has proposed that we should buy the special equipment needed to do the work ourselves in-house, thus making savings on the costs of the contract work. The equipment will cost £300,000 and we will also have to pay the following costs over the next five years:

	operators' wages £	repairs and maintenance £	other costs £
20-5	42,000	8,000	33,000
20-6	64,000	12,000	37,000
20-7	68,000	22,000	42,000
20-8	68,000	25,000	44,000
20-9	70,000	30,000	45,000

If we go ahead, the equipment will be bought at the end of this year ready for production to start in 20-5. At the end of 20-9 the equipment will have a scrap value of £10,000.

Please appraise this proposal from a financial viewpoint. I need to know the payback period and the net present value. As you know, the maximum required payback period is three years and, for net present value, we require a return of 14%.

Task 1

Use the working paper on the next page to calculate the net present value and the payback period of the proposed investment. Ignore inflation and calculate all money amounts to the nearest £.

Task 2

Write a report, dated 18 September 20-4, to the General Manager evaluating the proposal from a financial viewpoint. State any assumptions you have made in your analysis.

TOWAN KITCHENS LIMITED

Working paper for the financial appraisal of in-house worktop manufacture

CASH FLOWS

Year	Savings £	Total Costs £	Cash Flow £
20-4	–		
20-5			
20-6			
20-7			
20-8			
20-9			

DISCOUNTED CASH FLOW

Year	Cash Flow £	Discount Factor at 14%	Discounted Cash Flow £
20-4		1.000	
20-5		0.877	
20-6		0.769	
20-7		0.675	
20-8		0.592	
20-9		0.519	

Net Present Value (NPV)

PAYBACK PERIOD

Year	Cash Flow £	Cumulative Cash Flow £
20-4		
20-5		
20-6		
20-7		
20-8		
20-9		

Payback period =

10.5 Bridge Limited is an engineering company. It needs to replace an automated machine that is nearing the end of its working life.

Estimates have been made for the initial capital cost, sales income and operating costs of the replacement machine, which is expected to have a useful life of three years, at the end of which it will be sold for £15,000.

	Year 0 £000	Year 1 £000	Year 2 £000	Year 3 £000
Capital expenditure	75			
Disposal				15
Other cash flows:				
Sales revenue		65	80	55
Operating costs		30	35	35

The company appraises capital investment projects using a 10% cost of capital.

(a) **Complete the table below and calculate the net present value of the proposed replacement machine (to the nearest £000).**

	Year 0 £000	Year 1 £000	Year 2 £000	Year 3 £000
Capital expenditure				
Disposal				
Sales revenue				
Operating costs				
Net cash flows				
PV factors	1.0000	0.9091	0.8264	0.7513
Discounted cash flows				
Net present value				

Tick to show if the net present value is

positive	
negative	

or

(b) **Calculate the payback period of the proposed replacement machine to the nearest whole month.**

The payback period is _____ year(s) and _____ months.

10.6 You are an accounts assistant at Wentworth Limited. You have been given the task of investigating the cost the company pays for its telephone and internet service, with a view to reducing costs. You have contacted two different suppliers and, over a contract period of three years, you have estimated the annual costs as follows:

	Supplier 1 AtlanticTel £	Supplier 2 Speed Tel £
Year 1	3,500	3,000
Year 2	4,000	3,000
Year 3	4,000	5,500

Wentworth Limited uses a 12% cost of capital to appraise its future costs.

(a) **Complete the table below and calculate the net present cost of the contracts offered by the two suppliers (to the nearest £).**

	PV factors	Supplier 1 AtlanticTel		Supplier 2 Speed Tel	
		Cost £	Discounted cash flows £	Cost £	Discounted cash flows £
Year 1	0.8929	3,500	( )	3,000	( )
Year 2	0.7972	4,000	( )	3,000	( )
Year 3	0.7118	4,000	( )	5,500	( )
NET PRESENT COST		( )			( )

(b) **Tick to indicate which supplier Wentworth Limited should choose.**

✔

AtlanticTel	
Speed Tel	

Answers to chapter activities

Chapter activities – answers
1 An introduction to cost accounting

1.1

Statement	Financial accounting ✔	Cost accounting ✔
reports relate to what has happened in the past	✔	
may be required by law	✔	
gives estimates of costs and income for the future		✔
may be made public	✔	
gives up-to-date reports which can be used for controlling the business		✔
is used by people outside the business	✔	
is designed to meet the requirements of people inside the business		✔
shows details of the expected costs of materials, labour and expenses		✔
records accurate amounts, not estimates	✔	

1.2   rent of premises

1.3   raw materials to make the product

1.4   **(a)**

> **MERRETT MANUFACTURING LIMITED**
> **Total cost statement for the year ended 31 December 20-3**
>
> | | £ | £ |
> |---|---|---|
> | Direct materials | | 52,170 |
> | Direct labour | | 73,960 |
> | Direct expenses | | 4,890 |
> | PRIME COST | | 131,020 |
> | *Production overheads* | | |
> | Rent and rates of factory | 8,240 | |
> | Supervisors' wages | 35,130 | |
> | Depreciation of factory machinery | 6,250 | |
> | Electricity of factory | 5,940 | |
> | Sundry factory expenses | 2,860 | |
> | | | 58,420 |
> | PRODUCTION COST | | 189,440 |
> | *Non-production overheads* | | |
> | Administration costs: | | |
> | Rent and rates of office | 4,290 | |
> | Salaries of office staff | 45,730 | |
> | Depreciation of office equipment | 3,750 | |
> | Sundry office expenses | 1,340 | |
> | | | 55,110 |
> | TOTAL COST | | 244,550 |

Note: it has been assumed in the cost statement that all the raw materials used in the factory are direct materials

(b)

> **MERRETT MANUFACTURING LIMITED**
> **Income statement for the year ended 31 December 20-3**
>
> | | | £ |
> |---|---|---|
> | | Sales revenue | 286,320 |
> | *less* | Total cost | 244,550 |
> | | PROFIT | 41,770 |

1.5

REPORT

To: The Partners
From: Accounts Assistant
Date: today

Costs and income for last year
I report on the details of the costs and income for last year of each office of the practice. Details are as follows:

	Triangle	South Toynton	St Faiths
Cost Centre	£000	£000	£000
• materials	75	70	80
• labour	550	650	730
• expenses	82	69	89
• total	707	789	899
Profit Centre			
Income	950	869	1,195
less Costs (see above)	707	789	899
Profit	243	80	296
Investment Centre			
Profit (see above)	243	80	296
Investment	750	900	1,150
Expressed as a percentage	32%	9%	26%

Sheffield City College Library

1.6

Cost item	Classification (write your answer)
Insurance of buildings	indirect expense
Salaries of office staff	indirect labour
Zip fasteners	direct materials
Electricity	indirect expense*
Wages of factory supervisors	indirect labour
Pay of machine operators	direct labour
Consignment of blue denim	direct materials
Stationery for the office	indirect materials
Television advertising	indirect expense
Oil for production machines	indirect materials
Fuel for delivery vans	indirect materials
Wages of canteen staff	indirect labour

* The cost of electricity has been classified above as an indirect expense. This is often the case because it is not worthwhile analysing the cost of power for each unit of production. Where machines are used that take a lot of power, meters are often fitted to each machine so that costs may be identified and allocated to production as a direct expense. Whichever treatment – indirect expense or direct expense – it is important that it is applied consistently.

1.7

Cost item	Total cost	Prime cost	Production overheads	Admin-istration costs	Selling and distribution costs
	£	£	£	£	£
Wages of employees working on pre-fabrication line	19,205	19,205			
Supervisors' salaries	5,603		5,603		
Materials for making pre-fabricated panels	10,847	10,847			
Cleaning materials for factory machinery	315		315		
Sundry factory expenses	872		872		
Salaries of office staff	6,545			6,545	
Repairs to sales staff cars	731				731
Depreciation of office equipment	200			200	
Magazine advertising	1,508				1,508
Sundry office expenses	403			403	
Hire of display stands used at garden centres	500				500
Office stationery	276			276	
TOTALS	47,005	30,052	6,790	7,424	2,739

2 Chapter activities – answers
Materials costs

2.1   100 boxes

2.2

DATE 20-3	DESCRIPTION	FIFO £	AVCO £
21 June	Total issue value*	6,350	6,450
30 June	Total closing inventory value†	1,175	1,075

Workings:

* FIFO:	2,000 units issued at £2.00 per unit	=	£4,000
	1,000 units issued at £2.35 per unit	=	£2,350
			£6,350

AVCO:	(£4,000 + £3,525) ÷ 3,500 units	=	£2.15 per unit
	3,000 units issued at £2.15 per unit	=	£6,450

† FIFO:	500 units at £2.35 per unit	=	£1,175
AVCO:	500 units at £2.15 per unit	=	£1,075

2.3   (a)

INVENTORY RECORD: FIFO								
Product: Material Wye								
Date	**Receipts**			**Issues**			**Balance**		
20-1	Quantity (kgs)	Cost per kg	Total Cost	Quantity (kgs)	Cost per kg	Total Cost	Quantity (kgs)	Cost per kg	Total Cost
		£	£		£	£		£	£
1 Aug	Balance						5,000	5.00	25,000
10 Aug	2,000	5.25	10,500				5,000	5.00	25,000
							2,000	5.25	10,500
							7,000		35,500
18 Aug		3,000	5.50	16,500			5,000	5.00	25,000
							2,000	5.25	10,500
							3,000	5.50	16,500
							10,000		52,000
23 Aug				5,000	5.00	25,000			
				2,000	5.25	10,500			
				1,000	5.50	5,500	2,000	5.50	11,000

INVENTORY RECORD: AVCO								
Product: Material Zed								
Date	**Receipts**			**Issues**			**Balance**		
20-1	Quantity (kgs)	Cost per kg	Total Cost	Quantity (kgs)	Cost per kg	Total Cost	Quantity (kgs)	Cost per kg	Total Cost
		£	£		£	£		£	£
1 Aug	Balance						10,000	4.00	40,000
6 Aug	5,000	4.30	21,500				10,000	4.00	40,000
							5,000	4.30	21,500
							15,000	4.10	61,500
19 Aug	6,000	4.45	26,700				15,000	4.10	61,500
							6,000	4.45	26,700
							21,000	4.20	88,200
24 Aug				12,000	4.20	50,400	9,000	4.20	37,800

(b)   Valuation at 31 August 20-1:

material Wye   £10,000   (net realisable value)

material Zed   £37,800   (cost price)

£47,800

2.4   (a)

INVENTORY RECORD: FIFO

Product: Photocopying paper (reams)

Date	Receipts			Issues			Balance		
20-8	Quantity (reams)	Cost per ream £	Total Cost £	Quantity (reams)	Cost per ream £	Total Cost £	Quantity (reams)	Cost per ream £	Total Cost £
1 Feb	Balance						100	2.00	200
5 Feb				50	2.00	100	50	2.00	100
10 Feb	150	2.20	330				50	2.00	100
							150	2.20	330
							200		430
15 Feb				50	2.00	100			
				50	2.20	110	100	2.20	220
18 Feb	200	2.30	460				100	2.20	220
							200	2.30	460
							300		680
24 Feb				100	2.20	220			
				20	2.30	46	180	2.30	414

(b)

INVENTORY RECORD: AVCO

Product: Photocopying paper (reams)

Date	Receipts			Issues			Balance		
20-8	Quantity (reams)	Cost per ream £	Total Cost £	Quantity (reams)	Cost per ream £	Total Cost £	Quantity (reams)	Cost per ream £	Total Cost £
1 Feb	Balance						100	2.00	200
5 Feb				50	2.00	100	50	2.00	100
10 Feb	150	2.20	330				50	2.00	100
							150	2.20	330
							200	2.15	430
15 Feb				100	2.15	215	100	2.15	215
18 Feb	200	2.30	460				100	2.15	215
							200	2.30	460
							300	2.25	675
24 Feb				120	2.25	270	180	2.25	405

2.5 £10,900

2.6 **Task 1**

INVENTORY RECORD: FIFO								
Product: White plastic								
Date	Receipts			Issues			Balance	
	Quantity (kgs)	Cost per kg £	Total Cost £	Quantity (kgs)	Cost per kg £	Total Cost £	Quantity (kgs)	Total Cost £
20-9								
Balance at 1 April							20,000	20,000
7 April	10,000	1.10	11,000				30,000	31,000
12 April				20,000 5,000 25,000	1.00 1.10	20,000 5,500 25,500	5,000	5,500
20 April	20,000	1.20	24,000				5,000 20,000 25,000	5,500 24,000 29,500
23 April				5,000 10,000 15,000	1.10 1.20	5,500 12,000 17,500	10,000	12,000

Task 2

20-9	Code number	Debit £	Credit £
7 April	2000	£11,000	
7 April	3000		£11,000
12 April	2000		£25,500*
12 April	2100	£25,500	
20 April	2000	£24,000	
20 April	3000		£24,000
23 April	2000		£17,500**
23 April	2100	£17,500	

* £20,000 + £5,500   ** £5,500 + £12,000

2.7 (a)

$$Economic\ Order\ Quantity\ (EOQ) = \sqrt{\frac{2 \times 36{,}125\ kg \times £30}{£3}}$$

$$= \sqrt{\frac{2{,}167{,}500}{£3}}$$

$$= \sqrt{722{,}500}$$

$$= \underline{850\ kg}$$

(b) and (c)

Inventory record for metal grade X8

Date	Receipts			Issues			Balance	
	Quantity (kg)	Cost per kg	Total Cost	Quantity (kg)	Cost per kg	Total Cost	Quantity (kg)	Total Cost
		£	£		£	£		£
Balance as at 22 May							420	1,512
24 May	850	3.711	3,154				1,270	4,666
26 May				900	3.674	3,307	370	1,359
27 May	850	3.755	3,192				1,220	4,551
30 May				800	3.730	2,984	420	1,567

2.8

	Transaction	Account debited	Account credited
1.	Receipt of materials into inventory, paying immediately by BACS	Inventory	Bank
2.	Issue of materials from inventory to production	Production	Inventory
3.	Receipt of materials into inventory, purchased from a credit supplier	Inventory	Trade payables/ purchases ledger control
4.	Return of poor quality materials to a credit supplier	Trade payables/ purchases ledger control	Inventory
5.	Return of surplus materials from production to inventory	Inventory	Production

2.9

Statement	FIFO ✔	LIFO ✔	AVCO ✔
issues from inventory are from the most recent receipts		✔	
in times of rising prices, reported profits will usually be lower than with other methods		✔	
closing inventory is based on more recent costs of goods received	✔		
issues from inventory are from the earliest receipts	✔		
acceptable for tax purposes	✔		✔
closing inventory is valued at a weighted average cost			✔
permitted by IAS 2, *Inventories*	✔		✔
in times of rising prices the cost of sales figure will usually be lower than with other methods	✔		
closing inventory is based on older costs of goods received		✔	

3   Chapter activities – answers
Labour costs

3.1

Employee	Basic pay £	Overtime rate 1 £	Overtime rate 2 £	Gross pay for week £
L Constantinou	512.00	–	32.00	544.00
H Gunther	570.00	10.00	7.50	587.50
J White	428.40	17.00	10.20	455.60

3.2

Employee	Time rate £	Piecework rate £	Gross pay for week £
J Daniels	456.00	440.00	456.00
L Ho	402.50	422.50	422.50
T Turner	423.00	450.00	450.00

3.3

Employee	Time rate £	Bonus £	Gross pay for week £
H Hands	437.50	25.00	462.50
A Khan	434.75	0.00	434.75
T Shah	418.00	11.00	429.00
D Smith	512.00	9.60	521.60

3.4 Task 1

Dr		Wages Control Account		Cr
	£			£
Cash/bank (net wages)	8,000	Production (direct labour)		7,750
HM Revenue and Customs (income tax and NIC)	1,650	Production overheads (indirect labour)		1,500
Pension contributions	850	Non-production overheads (administration)		1,250
	10,500			10,500

Task 2

20-9	Code number	Debit £	Credit £
18 June	2100	7,750	
18 June	3100		7,750
18 June	2200	1,500	
18 June	3100		1,500
18 June	2300	1,250	
18 June	3100		1,250

3.5   (a)

Total cost of direct labour for February:

					£
2,600 hours	x	£10 per hour	=		26,000
400 hours	x	£15 (£10 + £5) per hour	=		6,000
3,000					32,000

(b)

Account name	Account code	Debit £	Account name	Account code	Credit £
Production – 'Porth boards'	2100	32,000	Wages control	4400	32,000

3.6

	Hours spent on production	Hours worked on indirect work	Notes	Basic pay £	Overtime premium £	Total pay £
Employee: S Patton			Profit Centre: Moulding			
Employee number: 617			Basic pay per hour: £12.00			
Monday	6	0		72	0	72
Tuesday	7	0		84	6	90
Wednesday	6	2	10 am-12 noon training	96	12	108
Thursday	8	0		96	12	108
Friday	6	1	8 am-9 am maintenance	84	6	90
Saturday	4	0		48	12	60
Sunday	2	0		24	24	48
Total	39	3		504	72	576

3.7

Statement	Time rate ✔	Piecework rate ✔	Bonus system ✔
The gross pay calculation is: hours worked x rate per hour	✔		
Method used for repetitive work where output is more important than quality		✔	
The gross pay calculation is: gross pay + proportion of the time saved			✔
The employer has to set time allowances for work done		✔	✔
Pay is not linked to output	✔		
Employees can earn more by working harder		✔	✔
There is no pressure on time, so quality of output should be maintained	✔		
The amount earned by employees varies with output		✔	✔
The gross pay calculation is: number of items produced x rate per item		✔	

Chapter activities – answers
Expenses

4

4.1

	capital expenditure ✔	revenue expenditure ✔
(a) building an extension to the administration office	✔	
(b) cleaning materials for factory machinery		✔
(c) repair of office photocopier		✔
(d) directors' salaries		✔
(e) carriage inwards on new machinery	✔	
(f) carriage inwards on raw materials		✔
(g) installation of computer system	✔	
(h) insurance of computer system		✔
(i) installation of special wiring for computer system	✔	

4.2

		DIRECT EXPENSES	INDIRECT EXPENSES	
			production overheads	non-production overheads
		✔	✔	✔
(a)	royalties paid to designer of product	✔		
(b)	straight-line depreciation of factory machinery		✔	
(c)	office electricity			✔
(d)	insurance of factory buildings		✔	
(e)	advertising			✔
(f)	rent on factory		✔	
(g)	units of output depreciation of factory machinery	✔		
(h)	factory manager's car expenses		✔	
(i)	sales department administration			✔

4.3   **Task 1**

Dr		General Expenses Account (3000)			Cr
20-4		£	20-4		£
30 Nov	Balance b/d	34,500	30 Nov	Production – Alpha	8,390
			30 Nov	Production – Beta	6,240
			30 Nov	Production overheads	13,850
			30 Nov	Non-production overheads – selling and distribution	3,170
			30 Nov	Non-production overheads – administration	2,850
		34,500			34,500

Task 2

20-4	Code number	Debit £	Credit £
30 Nov	1500	8,390	
30 Nov	3000		8,390
30 Nov	1600	6,240	
30 Nov	3000		6,240
30 Nov	2000	13,850	
30 Nov	3000		13,850
30 Nov	2500	3,170	
30 Nov	3000		3,170
30 Nov	2600	2,850	
30 Nov	3000		2,850

4.4

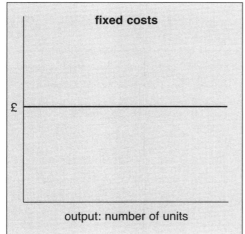

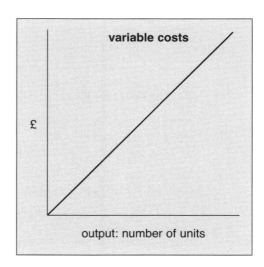

4.5

		fixed ✔	semi-variable ✔	variable ✔
(a)	rent of business premises	✔		
(b)	week's hire of machinery at £100 per week for one particular job	✔		
(c)	telephone system with a fixed line rental and a cost per call		✔	
(d)	supervisor's wages	✔		
(e)	reducing balance depreciation	✔		
(f)	production-line employees paid a basic wage, with a bonus linked to output		✔	
(g)	royalty paid to author for each book sold			✔
(h)	accountant's fees	✔		
(i)	raw materials used in production			✔

4.6   •   high output   30,000 units   £500,000

        less   low output   20,000 units   £350,000

        equals   difference   10,000 units   £150,000

   •   amount of variable cost per unit:

           $\dfrac{£150,000}{10,000}$ = £15 variable cost per unit

   •   at 20,000 units of output the cost structure is:

                   total cost   £350,000

        less   variable costs (20,000 units x £15 per unit)   £300,000

        equals   fixed costs   £ 50,000

   •   check at 30,000 units of output when the cost structure is:

                   variable costs (30,000 units x £15 per unit)   £450,000

        add   fixed costs (as above)   £ 50,000

        equals   total costs   £500,000

        Fixed costs, at these levels of output are   **£50,000**

4.7

20-2	FORECAST REVENUE AND COSTS		
UNITS PRODUCED AND SOLD	12,000	15,000	20,000
	£	£	£
Sales revenue	144,000	180,000	240,000
Variable costs			
Materials	36,000	45,000	60,000
Labour	24,000	30,000	40,000
Expenses	6,000	7,500	10,000
	66,000	82,500	110,000
Fixed costs			
Labour	18,500	18,500	18,500
Overheads	25,250	25,250	25,250
	43,750	43,750	43,750
Total cost	109,750	126,250	153,750
Total profit	34,250	53,750	86,250
Cost per unit (to 2 decimal places)	9.15	8.42	7.69
Profit per unit (to 2 decimal places)	2.85	3.58	4.31

Tutorial notes

- Sales revenue per unit is calculated at £12.00 (ie £144,000 ÷ 12,000 units)
- Variable costs per unit are:
  - materials, £3.00 (ie £36,000 ÷ 12,000 units)
  - labour, £2.00
  - expenses, £0.50
- Fixed costs remain fixed at the higher levels of output
- The costs at higher levels of output are on the basis that
  - there is a linear relationship for variable costs
  - there are no stepped fixed costs
- The fall in cost per unit as output increases occurs because the fixed costs are being spread over a greater number of units, ie the fixed cost per unit falls
- As cost per unit falls, so profit per unit increases (always provided that the selling price per unit can be maintained)

4.8

Batches produced and sold	1,000	1,500	1,800
	£	£	£
Sales revenue	45,000	67,500	81,000
Variable costs:			
• Direct materials	10,000	15,000	18,000
• Direct labour	12,000	18,000	21,600
• Overheads	8,000	12,000	14,400
Semi-variable costs:	4,000		
• Variable element		3,000	3,600
• Fixed element		2,000	2,000
Total cost	34,000	50,000	59,600
Total profit	11,000	17,500	21,400
Profit per batch (to 2 decimal places)	11.00	11.67	11.89

5 Chapter activities – answers
Overheads

5.1

OVERHEAD ANALYSIS		
January 20-7		
	Accountancy Department	Management Department
Budgeted total overheads (£)	15,884	19,855
Budgeted teaching hours	722	1,045
Budgeted overhead absorption rate (£)	22	19

OVERHEAD ANALYSIS		
Course: Finance for Managers		
	Accountancy Department	Management Department
Teaching hours	45	20
Budgeted overhead absorption rate (£)	22	19
Overhead absorbed by course (£)	990	380

5.2

WYEVALE PROCESSING LIMITED
BUDGETED PRODUCTION OVERHEAD SCHEDULE
for next month

Budgeted overhead	Basis of apportionment	Totals £	Processing £	Packing £	Quality Assurance £	Stores £	Maintenance £
Rent and rates	Floor area	4,500	1,200	1,575	375	600	750
Supervisors' salaries	Number of employees	3,690	1,230	1,722	246	246	246
Depreciation of equipment	Equipment usage	2,640	1,800	600	240		
Canteen costs	Number of employees	720	240	336	48	48	48
TOTAL		11,550	4,470	4,233	909	894	1,044

5.3

	Day care ward £	Surgical ward £	Operating theatre £	Administration £	Totals £
Overheads	28,750	42,110	32,260	9,075	112,195
Reapportion Administration	1,650	4,125	3,300	(9,075)	
Reapportion Operating theatre	20,320	15,240	(35,560)		
Total overheads to patient wards	50,720	61,475			112,195

5.4   Task 1

Budgeted overheads for four weeks ended 28 April 20-2	Basis of apportion-ment	Totals £	New Car Sales £	Used Car Sales £	Servicing £	Administration £
Depreciation of non-current assets	Carrying amount	8,400	2,100	1,260	4,200	840
Rent	Floor space	10,000	4,000	3,000	2,000	1,000
Other property overheads	Floor space	4,500	1,800	1,350	900	450
Staff costs	Allocated	35,295	11,080	7,390	9,975	6,850
Administration overheads	Allocated	3,860				3,860
		62,055	18,980	13,000	17,075	13,000
Administration			2,600	3,900	6,500	(13,000)
		62,055	21,580	16,900	23,575	–

Task 2

Budgeted overhead absorption rate for the servicing centre:

£23,575 ÷ 1,025 hours =

£23.00 per direct labour hour

5.5

	Basis of apportionment	Moulding £	Finishing £	Maintenance £	Stores £	Admin £	Totals £
Depreciation of equipment	Carrying amount* of equipment	3,000	1,200				4,200
Power for production machinery	Power usage	1,800	240				2,040
Rent and rates	Floor space			1,300	2,080	3,120	6,500
Light and heat	Floor space			550	880	1,320	2,750
Indirect labour	Allocated			38,550	29,850	51,250	119,650
Totals		4,800	1,440	40,400	32,810	55,690	135,140
Reapportion Maintenance		30,300	10,100	(40,400)			
Reapportion Stores		19,686	13,124		(32,810)		
Reapportion Administration		27,845	27,845			(55,690)	
Total overheads to production centres		82,631	52,509				135,140

* net book value

5.6   **1.**   moulding £9 per hour; finishing £22 per hour

2.   moulding £16 per hour; finishing £15 per hour

3.   moulding under absorbed £1,600; finishing over absorbed £900

5.7

Dr   **Production Overheads Account: Kitchen Department**   Cr

	£		£
Bank (overheads incurred)	5,000	Production	5,600
Income statement (over absorption)	600		
	5,600		5,600

Dr   **Production Overheads Account: Canning Department**   Cr

	£		£
Bank (overheads incurred)	3,500	Production	3,200
		Income statement (under absorption)	300
	3,500		3,500

20-6	Code number	Debit £	Credit £
16 June	2000	£5,600	
16 June	2100		£5,600
16 June	2000	£3,200	
16 June	2200		£3,200
16 June	2100	£600	
16 June	4000		£600
16 June	4000	£300	
16 June	2200		£300

6 Chapter activities – answers
Methods of costing

6.1 Task 1

	number of copies		
JOB NO 12345 **Poetry book for John Dun**	500	1,000	2,000
	£	£	£
Fixed Costs			
Setting up machine	60.00	60.00	60.00
Artwork	84.00	84.00	84.00
Page setting	300.00	300.00	300.00
Direct Materials			
Paper	200.00	400.00	800.00
Other printing consumables	100.00	200.00	400.00
Direct Labour	65.00	130.00	260.00
Production Overheads			
(80% of direct labour costs)	52.00	104.00	208.00
TOTAL COST	861.00	1,278.00	2,112.00
Profit (25% of total cost)	215.25	319.50	528.00
SELLING PRICE	1,076.25	1,597.50	2,640.00

Task 2

	Cost per book to author:
500 copies	£2.15
1,000 copies	£1.60
2,000 copies	£1.32

6.2

Cost element	Costs	Completed Units	Work-in-progress			Total Equivalent Units	Cost per Unit	WIP valuation
			Units	% complete	Equivalent Units			
	A	B	C	D	E	F	G	H
					C x D	B + E	A ÷ F	E x G
	£						£	£
Direct materials	10,725	2,750	500	100	500	3,250	3.30	1,650
Direct labour	6,600	2,750	500	50	250	3,000	2.20	550
Production overheads	3,900	2,750	500	50	250	3,000	1.30	325
Total	21,225						6.80	2,525

6.3

Dr				Process Account				Cr
	Quantity (litres)	Unit cost	Total cost		Quantity (litres)	Unit cost	Total cost	
		£	£			£	£	
Materials	65,000	0.30	19,500	Normal loss	5,000	0.05	250	
Labour		0.20	13,000	Finished goods	60,000	0.70	42,000	
Overheads		0.15	9,750					
	65,000		42,250		65,000		42,250	

Dr		Normal Loss Account		Cr
	£			£
Process account	250	Bank/receivables		250

Tutorial note:

The cost per unit of the expected output is:

$$\frac{£42,250 - £250}{60,000 \text{ litres}} = £0.70 \text{ per litre}$$

6.4

Dr				Process Account				Cr
	Quantity	Unit cost	Total cost		Quantity	Unit cost	Total cost
	(kilos)	£	£		(kilos)	£	£
Materials	84,000	0.20	16,800	Normal loss	4,000	0.20	800
Labour		0.15	12,600	Finished goods	81,000	0.41	33,210
Overheads		0.05	4,200				
			33,600				
Abnormal gain	1,000	0.41	410				
	85,000		34,010		85,000		34,010

Dr		Normal Loss Account		Cr
	£			£
Process account	800	Bank/receivables		600
		Abnormal gain account		*200
	800			800

Dr		Abnormal Gain Account		Cr
	£			£
Normal loss account	*200	Process account		410

* 1,000 kilos at 20p per kilo

Tutorial note:

The cost per unit of the expected output is:

$$\frac{£33,600 - £800}{80,000 \text{ kilos}} = £0.41 \text{ per kilo}$$

6.5

Dr	Quantity	Unit cost	Total cost	**Process 1 Account**	Quantity	Unit cost	Total cost
	(kilos)	£	£		(kilos)	£	£
Materials	5,000	0.40	2,000	Normal loss (5%)	250	0.20	50
Labour		0.20	1,000	Transfer to			
Overheads		0.10	500	process 2	4,500	0.73	3,268
							3,318
				Abnormal loss	250	0.73	182
	5,000		3,500		5,000		3,500

Dr	Quantity	Unit cost	Total cost	**Process 2 Account**	Quantity	Unit cost	Total cost
	(kilos)	£	£		(kilos)	£	£
Transfer from				Normal loss (3%)	135	0.40	54
process 1	4,500	0.73	3,268	Finished goods	4,400	1.15	5,054
Labour		0.25	1,125				
Overheads		0.15	675				
			5,068				
Abnormal gain	35	1.15	40				
	4,535		5,108		4,535		5,108

Dr		**Normal Loss Account**	Cr
	£		£
Process 1 account	50	Bank/receivables	50
Process 2 account	54	Bank/receivables	40
		Abnormal gain account	*14
	104		104

Dr		**Abnormal Loss Account**		Cr
	£			£
Process 1 account	182	Bank/receivables (250 kilos x 20p)		50

Dr		**Abnormal Gain Account**		Cr
	£			£
Normal loss account	*14	Process 2 account		40

* 35 kilos x 40p per kilo

Tutorial notes:

- In process 1, the cost per unit of the expected output is:

$$\frac{£3,500 - £50}{4,750 \text{ kilos}} = £0.73 \text{ per kilo}$$

- In process 2, the cost per unit of the expected output is:

$$\frac{£5,068 - £54}{4,365 \text{ kilos}} = £1.15 \text{ per kilo}$$

6.6   (a)

Description	kilos	Unit cost £	Total cost £	Description	kilos	Unit cost £	Total cost £
Material ZC6	300	1.60	480	Normal loss	100	0.50	50
Material ZC8	1,500	0.80	1,200	Output	1,900	7.50	14,250
Material ZC10	200	1.50	300				
Labour			6,720				
Overheads			5,600				
	2,000		14,300		2,000		14,300

(b)

	Debit ✓	Credit ✓
Process	✓	
Abnormal gain		✓

7 Chapter activities – answers
Marginal and absorption costing

7.1

Marginal cost per seat	£55.00
Absorption cost per seat	£80.00
Profit or loss if 4,000 seats are sold	£80,000.00

Workings:

Marginal cost per seat	£
Direct materials	25.00
Direct labour	30.00
MARGINAL COST	55.00

Absorption cost per seat	£
Direct materials	25.00
Direct labour	30.00
Fixed production overheads £100,000 ÷ 4,000 seats	25.00
ABSORPTION COST	80.00

OUTDOOR LIMITED
INCOME STATEMENT: 4,000 SEATS

	£	£
Sales revenue (4,000 x £100)		400,000
Direct materials (4,000 x £25)	100,000	
Direct labour (4,000 x £30)	120,000	
Fixed production overheads	100,000	
TOTAL COST		320,000
PROFIT		80,000

7.2 (a)

STRELLIS LIMITED

INCOME STATEMENT FOR THE MONTH ENDED 30 JUNE 20-5

	MARGINAL COSTING		ABSORPTION COSTING	
	£	£	£	£
Sales revenue 3,500 units at £10 each		35,000		35,000
Variable costs				
Direct materials at £2.50 each	10,000		10,000	
Direct labour at £3.00 each	12,000		12,000	
	22,000			
Less Closing inventory (marginal cost*)				
500 units at £5.50 each	2,750			
	19,250			
Fixed production overheads	15,000		15,000	
			37,000	
Less Closing inventory (absorption cost*)				
500 units at £9.25 each			4,625	
Less Cost of sales		34,250		32,375
PROFIT		750		2,625

* Closing inventory is calculated on the basis of this year's costs:

marginal costing, variable costs only, ie £2.50 + £3.00 = £5.50 per unit x 500 units = £2,750

absorption costing, variable and fixed costs,
ie £37,000 ÷ 4,000 units = £9.25 per unit x 500 units = £4,625

(b)   The difference in the profit figures is caused only by the closing inventory figures: £2,750 under marginal costing, and £4,625 under absorption costing. With marginal costing, the full amount of the fixed production overheads has been charged in this year's income statement; by contrast, under absorption costing, part of the fixed production overheads (here £15,000 x 12.5%* = £1,875) has been carried forward in the inventory valuation.

* 500 units of closing inventory out of 4,000 units manufactured

7.3 direct materials

7.4 prime cost

7.5

	Manufacturing account ✔	Income statement ✔
salaries of sales staff		✔
wages of production-line employees	✔	
royalty paid to designer of product	✔	
straight-line depreciation of factory machinery	✔	
factory power costs	✔	
re-decoration of administration office		✔
interest on bank loan		✔

7.6

MIDDLETON MANUFACTURING COMPANY
MANUFACTURING ACCOUNT AND INCOME STATEMENT
for the year ended 31 December 20-5

	£	£
Opening inventory of direct materials		25,250
Add Purchases of direct materials		75,340
		100,590
Less Closing inventory of direct materials		29,610
DIRECT MATERIALS USED		70,980
Direct labour		54,690
PRIME COST		125,670
Add Production (factory) overheads:		
Indirect labour	22,330	
Rent and rates	7,380	
Power	4,250	
Depreciation of factory machinery	2,500	
Repairs to factory buildings	1,870	
Sundry factory expenses	1,140	
		39,470
PRODUCTION (FACTORY) COST OF GOODS MANUFACTURED		165,140
Sales revenue		286,940
Opening inventory of finished goods	12,380	
Production (factory) cost of goods manufactured	165,140	
	177,520	
Less Closing inventory of finished goods	11,490	
COST OF SALES		166,030
Gross profit		120,910
Less Non-production overheads		46,730
Profit for the year		74,180

7.7

RASHLEIGH MANUFACTURING LIMITED
MANUFACTURING ACCOUNT AND INCOME STATEMENT
for the year ended 30 June 20-7

	£	£
Opening inventory of direct materials		22,840
Add Purchases of direct materials		127,330
		150,170
Less Closing inventory of direct materials		25,290
DIRECT MATERIALS USED		124,880
Direct labour		86,520
PRIME COST		211,400
Add Production (factory) overheads:		
Indirect labour	53,210	
Rent and rates	18,420	
Power	9,760	
Heat and light	2,150	
Sundry expenses and maintenance	4,720	
Depreciation of plant and machinery	15,000	
		103,260
		314,660
Add Opening inventory of work-in-progress		10,470
		325,130
Less Closing inventory of work-in-progress		9,630
PRODUCTION (FACTORY) COST OF GOODS MANUFACTURED		315,500
Sales revenue		525,460
Opening inventory of finished goods	33,640	
Production (factory) cost of goods manufactured	315,500	
	349,140	
Less Closing inventory of finished goods	32,790	
COST OF SALES		316,350
Gross profit		209,110
Less Non-production overheads:		
Rent and rates	6,140	
Administration salaries	77,280	
Advertising	27,430	
Office expenses	8,310	
Depreciation of office equipment	5,000	
		124,160
Profit for the year		84,950

8   Chapter activities – answers
Aspects of budgeting

8.1   direct materials variance £200 favourable; direct labour variance £350 adverse

8.2   direct materials £6,160; direct labour £9,020

8.3

Cause of variance	Adverse ✔	Favourable ✔
decrease in cost of direct materials		✔
more materials are wasted	✔	
more expensive direct materials are used	✔	
specifications are changed to use cheaper materials		✔
a cheaper grade of direct labour is employed		✔
machine speed is increased		✔
during the recession direct labour agrees to work an extra hour a week for no pay		✔
the cost of power for the machines increases	✔	
a fluctuation in exchange rates increases the cost of imported raw materials	✔	
selling prices are reduced	✔	
there is a decrease in the volume of output sold	✔	

8.4

BUDGET REPORT				
	Flexed budget	**Actual**	**Variance**	**Favourable (F) or Adverse (A)**
Output level	95%			
	£	£	£	
Direct materials	3,420	3,500	80	A
Direct labour	8,930	9,350	420	A
Overheads	7,500	7,300	200	F
TOTAL	19,850	20,150	300	A

8.5

	Flexed budget	**Actual**	**Variance**	**Favourable (F) or Adverse (A)**
Volume sold	45,000	45,000		
	£000	£000	£000	
Sales revenue	1,080	1,050	30	A
Less costs:				
Direct materials	270	260	10	F
Direct labour	360	410	50	A
Overheads	350	330	20	F
Operating profit	100	50	50	A

8.6

	Flexed budget	Actual	Variance	Favourable (F) or Adverse (A)
Volume sold	6,450	6,450		
	£000	£000	£000	
Sales revenue	903	910	7	F
Less costs:				
Direct materials	172	190	18	A
Direct labour	258	255	3	F
Overheads	280	300	20	A
Operating profit	193	165	28	A

9 Chapter activities – answers
Short-term decisions

9.1 (a)

units of output (litres)	fixed costs	variable costs	total cost	sales revenue	profit/(loss)
	£	£	£	£	£
0	750	0	750	0	(750)
5,000	750	6,000	6,750	6,250	(500)
10,000	750	12,000	12,750	12,500	(250)
15,000	750	18,000	18,750	18,750	0
16,000	750	19,200	19,950	20,000	50
17,000	750	20,400	21,150	21,250	100
18,000	750	21,600	22,350	22,500	150
19,000	750	22,800	23,550	23,750	200
20,000	750	24,000	24,750	25,000	250

(b)

Margin of safety at sales of 18,000 litres	3,000 litres	17%

Tutorial note:

current output – break-even output = 18,000 litres – 15,000 litres = 3,000 litres

$$\frac{\text{current output – break-even output}}{\text{current output}} \times \frac{100}{1}$$

$$= \frac{18,000 \text{ litres} - 15,000 \text{ litres}}{18,000 \text{ litres}} = 16.67\% = 17\%$$

9.2   (a)   1,500 units

(b)   £33,000

(c)

Units of AN02 sold	2,000	2,500
Margin of safety (units)	500	1,000
Margin of safety (percentage)	25	40

(d)   2,250 units

(e)   the break-even point will decrease and the margin of safety will increase

9.3 **Task 1**

the contribution sales (CS) ratio	0.25 or 25%
the break-even point in units	20,000 units
the break-even point in sales revenue	£400,000
the margin of safety in units at the forecast output	5,000 units
the number of units to generate a profit of £50,000	30,000 units

Workings:

- contribution sales (CS) ratio

$$\frac{\text{contribution (£)}}{\text{selling price (£)}} = \frac{£5^*}{£20} = 0.25 \text{ or } 25\%$$

* selling price £20 – variable cost £15

- break-even point in units

$$\frac{\text{fixed costs (£)}}{\text{contribution per unit (£)}} = \frac{£100,000}{£5} = 20,000 \text{ units}$$

- break-even point in sales revenue

$$\frac{\text{fixed costs (£)}}{\text{CS ratio}} = \frac{£100,000}{0.25} = £400,000$$

check: 20,000 units x selling price £20 per unit = £400,000

- margin of safety at output of 25,000 units

$$\frac{\text{current output} - \text{break-even output}}{\text{current output}} = \frac{25,000 - 20,000}{25,000} \times \frac{100}{1}$$

= 20%, or 5,000 units

- number of units to generate a profit of £50,000

$$\frac{\text{fixed costs (£) + target profit (£)}}{\text{contribution per unit (£)}} = \frac{£100,000 + £50,000}{£5} = 30,000 \text{ units}$$

Task 2

Calculate the profit at:

the forecast output	£25,000
the maximum output	£75,000

Workings:

		forecast output (25,000 units) £	maximum output (35,000 units) £
	sales revenue (at £20 each)	500,000	700,000
less	variable costs (at £15 each)	375,000	525,000
equals	contribution (to fixed costs and profit)	125,000	175,000
less	monthly fixed costs	100,000	100,000
equals	forecast profit for month	25,000	75,000

9.4 **Task 1**

Product	'People'	'Animals'	'Birds'
Selling price per unit	60	27.50	17.50
Less: Unit variable costs			
Direct materials	5	3	2
Direct labour	15	5	3.33
Variable overheads	10	4.50	2.96
Contribution per unit	30	15	9.21

Task 2

Break-even point for the 'People' range is:

$$\frac{\text{fixed costs (£)}}{\text{contribution per unit (£)}} = \frac{£45,400}{£30} = \underline{\underline{1,514 \text{ units}}}$$

Task 3

Product	'People'	'Animals'	'Birds'
Contribution per unit	£30	£15	£9.21
Labour hours per unit	1.5	0.5	0.33
Contribution per labour hour	£20	£30	£27.63

Task 4

- Labour hours are the limiting factor here, with only 2,800 hours available.
- To maximise profits, the company should maximise the contribution from each labour hour.
- The preferred order is 'Animals' (at £30 contribution per labour hour), 'Birds' (at £27.63), and 'People' (at £20).
- The company's production plan will be:

  'Animals', 2,000 units x 0.5 hours per unit = 1,000 hours

  'Birds', 2,700 units x 0.33 hours per unit = 900 hours

  'People', 600 units x 1.5 hours per unit   = <u>900</u> balance of hours available

                                                        <u>2,800</u> hours

Note that this production plan does not allow for full production of the 'People' range.

9.5   *Absorption cost*   £
     direct materials (per pair)   20.00
     direct labour (per pair)   18.00
     production overheads (fixed)   £200,000 ÷ 12,500 pairs   16.00
     ABSORPTION COST (per pair)   54.00

    Marginal cost   £
     direct materials (per pair)   20.00
     direct labour (per pair)   18.00
     MARGINAL COST (per pair)   38.00

Profit or loss at existing production of 12,500 pairs of boots, see below.

THE LAST COMPANY
income statements

	Existing production 12,500 pairs of boots £	Existing production + 2,500 pairs @ £45 each £	Existing production + 5,000 pairs @ £37 each £
Sales revenue (per year):			
12,500 pairs at £60 each	750,000	750,000	750,000
2,500 pairs at £45 each	–	112,500	–
5,000 pairs at £37 each	–	–	185,000
	750,000	862,500	935,000
Less production costs:			
Direct materials (£20 per pair)	250,000	300,000	350,000
Direct labour (£18 per pair)	225,000	270,000	315,000
Production overheads (fixed)	200,000	200,000	200,000
PROFIT	75,000	92,500	70,000

The conclusion is that the first special order should be accepted, and the second declined.

10 Chapter activities – answers
Long-term decisions

10.1 (a) payback period

	PROJECT ESS			PROJECT TEE	
Year	Cash Flow	Cumulative Cash Flow		Cash Flow	Cumulative Cash Flow
	£000	£000		£000	£000
0	(100)	(100)		(115)	(115)
1	40	(60)		50	(65)
2	60	–		35	(30)
3	20	20		30	–
4	20	40		30	30
5	*15	55		*37.5	67.5

* includes scrap value

As can be seen from the above table:

- Project Ess pays back after two years
- Project Tee pays back after three years

(b)   net present value

		PROJECT ESS		PROJECT TEE	
Year	Discount Factor	Cash Flow £000	Discounted Cash Flow £000	Cash Flow £000	Discounted Cash Flow £000
0	1.000	(100)	(100)	(115)	(115)
1	0.909	40	36.36	50	45.45
2	0.826	60	49.56	35	28.91
3	0.751	20	15.02	30	22.53
4	0.683	20	13.66	30	20.49
5	0.621	15	9.31	37.5	23.29
Net Present Value (NPV)			23.91		25.67

REPORT

To: Managing Director

From: Accounts Assistant

Date: Today

Capital investment projects: Ess and Tee

I have carried out an appraisal of these two projects, based on the information provided. I have used two techniques:

• payback

• net present value

The first of these, payback, sees how long it takes for the initial outlay of the project to be repaid by the net cash flow coming in. For Project Ess, the payback period is two years; for Project Tee, it is three years. Using this technique, Project Ess is more favourable.

Payback is an easy technique both to calculate and understand. However, it does have the disadvantage of ignoring all cash flows after the payback period. With these two projects, Tee has strong cash inflows in years 4 and 5, after the payback period (however, these could be a disadvantage if the project is likely to go out-of-date soon).

The net present value (NPV) technique relies on discounting relevant cash flows at an appropriate rate of return, which is 10 per cent for these projects. Net present value is a more sophisticated technique than payback in that it uses all cash flows and takes the timing of cash flows into account. However, the meaning of NPV is not always clear, and the rate of return required on the projects may vary over their life.

Project Tee has a higher NPV (but also a higher initial cost) at £25,670, when compared with Ess at £23,910. The fact that both figures are positive means that either project will be worthwhile. However, in view of the differing initial costs, it would be appropriate to calculate the internal rate of return, so that a comparison can be made directly between the two projects.

10.2 **(a)**

Year	Cash Flow £		Discount Factor 10%		Discounted Cash Flow £
Year 0	(55,000)	x	1.000	=	(55,000)
Year 1	19,376	x	0.909	=	17,613
Year 2	28,491	x	0.826	=	23,534
Year 3	21,053	x	0.751	=	15,811
			Net Present Value (NPV)	=	1,958

Year	Cash Flow £		Discount Factor 12%		Discounted Cash Flow £
Year 0	(55,000)	x	1.000	=	(55,000)
Year 1	19,376	x	0.893	=	17,303
Year 2	28,491	x	0.797	=	22,707
Year 3	21,053	x	0.712	=	14,990
			Net Present Value (NPV)	=	nil

Year	Cash Flow £		Discount Factor 14%		Discounted Cash Flow £
Year 0	(55,000)	x	1.000	=	(55,000)
Year 1	19,376	x	0.877	=	16,993
Year 2	28,491	x	0.769	=	21,910
Year 3	21,053	x	0.675	=	14,211
			Net Present Value (NPV)	=	(1,886)

(b)

- At an annual rate of return of 10%, the net present value is positive so it is worth going ahead with the project.

- At an annual rate of return of 12%, the net present value is nil, so 12% is the internal rate of return (IRR) of this project, ie the rate of return at which the present value of the cash inflows exactly balances the initial investment, that is 'breaks even'. As there is no positive net present value, the project will be rejected.

- At an annual rate of return of 14%, the net present value is negative, so the project will be rejected.

10.3   Task 1

CHESTER CARPET COMPANY LIMITED

Working paper for the financial appraisal of a new machine for the production department

DISCOUNTED CASH FLOW

Year	Cash Flow	Discount Factor at 10%	Discounted Cash Flow
	£		£
20-1	(65,000)	1.000	(65,000)
20-2	17,000	0.909	15,453
20-3	25,000	0.826	20,650
20-4	31,000	0.751	23,281
20-5	*28,000	0.683	19,124
Net Present Value (NPV)			13,508

* £24,000 + £4,000 scrap value

PAYBACK PERIOD

Year	Cash Flow	Cumulative Cash Flow	
	£	£	
20-1	(65,000)	(65,000)	
20-2	17,000	(48,000)	
20-3	25,000	(23,000)	
20-4	31,000	8,000	£23,000* required
20-5	28,000	36,000	

* £31,000 – £8,000

Payback period = 2 years + (£23,000/£31,000) = 2.7 years, ie 2 years and 9 months

Task 2

REPORT
To: General Manager
From: Accounts Assistant
Date: 24 November 20-1

Purchase of a new machine for the production department

I have carried out an appraisal of the above project. The proposal to purchase the new machine is acceptable from a financial viewpoint because it returns a positive net present value of £13,508 at a discount rate of 10%. This calculation assumes that all cash flows occur at the end of each year.

The payback period is during 20-4. If we assume even cash flows during the year, the payback period can be calculated as 2.7 years (or 2 years and 9 months) from the start. This is acceptable since it is shorter than the company requirement of three years, although there is not a great deal of room for error in the cash flow calculations.

10.4 Task 1

TOWAN KITCHENS LIMITED

Working paper for the financial appraisal of in-house worktop manufacture

CASH FLOWS

Year	Savings £	Total Costs £	Cash Flow £
20-4	–	(300,000)	(300,000)
20-5	200,000	(83,000)	117,000
20-6	200,000	(113,000)	87,000
20-7	200,000	(132,000)	68,000
20-8	200,000	(137,000)	63,000
20-9	200,000	*(135,000)	65,000

* costs total £145,000 less scrap value £10,000

Tutorial note: for 2005 to 2009 total costs are: operators' wages + repairs and maintenance + other costs

DISCOUNTED CASH FLOW

Year	Cash Flow £	Discount Factor at 14%	Discounted Cash Flow £
20-4	(300,000)	1.000	(300,000)
20-5	117,000	0.877	102,609
20-6	87,000	0.769	66,903
20-7	68,000	0.675	45,900
20-8	63,000	0.592	37,296
20-9	65,000	0.519	33,735
Net Present Value (NPV)			(13,557)

PAYBACK PERIOD

Year	Cash Flow £	Cumulative Cash Flow £	
20-4	(300,000)	(300,000)	
20-5	117,000	(183,000)	
20-6	87,000	(96,000)	
20-7	68,000	(28,000)	
20-8	63,000	35,000	£28,000* required
20-9	65,000	100,000	

* £63,000 – £35,000

Payback period = 3 years + (£28,000/£63,000) = 3.4 years, ie 3 years and 5 months

Task 2

REPORT
To: General Manager **From:** Accounts Assistant **Date:** 18 September 20-4
<u>Purchase of equipment to manufacture worktops</u> I have carried out an appraisal of the above project. Unfortunately, the proposal to purchase the new equipment is not acceptable from a financial viewpoint because it returns a negative net present value of £13,557 at a discount rate of 14%. This calculation assumes that all cash flows occur at the end of each year. At a lower rate of return, for example 10%, the project would be acceptable with a positive net present value. The payback period is during 20-8. If we assume even cash flows during the year, the payback period can be calculated as 3.4 years (or 3 years and 5 months) from the start. This is longer than the company requirement of three years, and so the project is not acceptable.

10.5   (a)

	Year 0 £000	Year 1 £000	Year 2 £000	Year 3 £000
Capital expenditure	75			
Disposal				15
Sales revenue		65	80	55
Operating costs		30	35	35
Net cash flows	(75)	35	45	35
PV factors	1.0000	0.9091	0.8264	0.7513
Discounted cash flows	(75)	32	37	26
Net present value	20			

positive	✔
or | negative | |

(b)   The payback period is 1 year(s) and 11 months.

10.6 (a)

	PV factors	Supplier 1 AtlanticTel		Supplier 2 Speed Tel	
		Cost	Discounted cash flows	Cost	Discounted cash flows
		£	£	£	£
Year 1	0.8929	3,500	(3,125)	3,000	(2,679)
Year 2	0.7972	4,000	(3,189)	3,000	(2,392)
Year 3	0.7118	4,000	(2,847)	5,500	(3,915)
NET PRESENT COST			(9,161)		(8,986)

(b)

AtlanticTel	
Speed Tel	✔

Costs and revenues

Practice assessment 1

- Each task of the Assessment is to be answered separately.
- This Assessment relates to the costs and revenues of Westlake Limited, a manufacturing business.

Section 1

Task 1.1

The following information is available for metal grade M5:

- Annual demand – 16,000 kilograms (kg)
- Annual holding cost per kilogram – £4
- Fixed ordering cost – £20

(a)   Calculate the Economic Order Quantity (EOQ) for M5.

> EOQ = ...kg

The inventory record shown below for metal grade M5 for the month of December has only been fully completed for the first three weeks of the month.

(b)   Complete the entries in the inventory record for the two receipts on 23 and 29 December that were ordered using the EOQ method.

(c)   Complete ALL entries in the inventory record for the two issues in the month and for the closing balance at the end of December using the FIFO method of issuing inventory.

Show the costs per kilogram (kg) in £ to 2 decimal places, and the total costs in whole £.

Inventory record for metal grade M5

Date	Receipts Quantity (kg)	Receipts Cost per kg £	Receipts Total Cost £	Issues Quantity (kg)	Issues Cost per kg £	Issues Total Cost £	Balance Quantity (kg)	Balance Total Cost £
Balance as at 22 December							350	840
23 December		2.50						
28 December				500				
29 December		2.60						
30 December				300				

Task 1.2

Westlake Limited uses the following accounts to record payroll transactions in its cost book-keeping system:

> – wages control
>
> – production
>
> – production overheads
>
> – non-production overheads

For each of the four transactions in the following table show the account which will be debited and the account which will be credited.

Transaction	Account debited	Account credited
1. Paid wages of direct labour employees		
2. Paid wages of factory supervisors		
3. Paid wages of office staff		
4. Correction of wages overpaid in error to factory supervisors		

Task 1.3

Below is a weekly time sheet for one of Westlake Limited's employees who is paid as follows:

• For a basic six-hour shift every day from Monday to Friday – basic pay

• For any overtime in excess of the basic six hours on any day from Monday to Friday – the extra hours are paid at time-and-a-half (basic pay plus an overtime premium equal to half of basic pay)

• For three contracted hours each Saturday morning – basic pay

• For any hours worked in excess of three hours on a Saturday – the extra hours are paid at double-time (basic pay plus an overtime premium equal to basic pay)

• For any hours worked on a Sunday – paid at double-time (basic pay plus an overtime premium equal to basic pay)

Complete the columns headed basic pay, overtime premium and total pay.

(Note: Zero figures should be entered in cells where appropriate; overtime pay is the premium amount paid for the extra hours worked.)

Employee's weekly time sheet for week ending 7 December

Employee:	S Wong		Profit Centre: Cutting			
Employee number:	HZ24		Basic pay per hour: £14.00			
	Hours spent on production	Hours worked on indirect work	Notes	Basic pay £	Overtime premium £	Total pay £
Monday	6	0		84	0	84
Tuesday	6	2	8 am -10 am maintenance	112	14	126
Wednesday	7	0		98	7	105
Thursday	4	3	9 am -12 noon training	98	7	105
Friday	7	1	2 pm - 3 pm first aid course	112	14	126
Saturday	4	0		56	14	70
Sunday	2	0		28	28	56
Total	36	6		588	84	672

Task 1.4

Westlake Limited's budgeted overheads for the next financial year are:

	£	£
Depreciation of production machinery		4,450
Power for production machinery		2,970
Rent and rates		8,550
Light and heat		2,250
Indirect labour costs:		
Maintenance	16,400	
Stores	30,300	
Administration	35,650	
Totals	82,350	18,220

The following information is also available:

Department	Net book value/ carrying amount of equipment	Production machinery power usage (KwH)	Floor space (square metres)	Number of employees
Production cost centres:				
Cutting	30,000	8,000		3
Finishing	20,000	2,000		2
Support cost centres:				
Maintenance			70	1
Stores			120	2
Administration			110	3
Total	50,000	10,000	300	11

Overheads are allocated or apportioned on the most appropriate basis. The total overheads of the support cost centres are then reapportioned to the two production centres, using the direct method.

•   80% of the maintenance cost centre's time is spent maintaining production machinery in the cutting production centre and the remainder in the finishing production centre.

•   The stores cost centre makes 70% of its issues to the cutting production centre, and 30% to the finishing production centre.

•   Administration supports the two production centres equally.

•   There is no reciprocal servicing between the three support cost centres.

Complete the apportionment table below using the data above.

	Basis of apportionment	Cutting £	Finishing £	Maintenance £	Stores £	Admin £	Totals £
Depreciation of production machinery							
Power for production machinery							
Rent and rates							
Light and heat							
Indirect labour							
Totals							
Reapportion Maintenance							
Reapportion Stores							
Reapportion Administration							
Total overheads to production centres							

Task 1.5

Next quarter Westlake Limited's budgeted overheads and activity levels are:

	Cutting	**Finishing**
Budgeted overheads (£)	18,900	10,450
Budgeted direct labour hours	1,350	950
Budgeted machine hours	2,100	1,045

(a) **What would be the budgeted overhead absorption rate for each department if this were set based on their both being heavily automated?**

	✔
cutting £9 per hour; finishing £10 per hour	
cutting £9 per hour; finishing £11 per hour	
cutting £14 per hour; finishing £10 per hour	
cutting £14 per hour; finishing £11 per hour	

(b) **What would be the budgeted overhead absorption rate for each department if this were set based on their both being labour intensive?**

	✔
cutting £9 per hour; finishing £10 per hour	
cutting £9 per hour; finishing £11 per hour	
cutting £14 per hour; finishing £10 per hour	
cutting £14 per hour; finishing £11 per hour	

Additional data

At the end of the quarter actual overheads incurred were found to be:

	Cutting	Finishing
Actual overheads (£)	19,300	9,850

(c) **Assuming that exactly the same amount of overheads was absorbed as budgeted, what were the budgeted under or over absorptions in the quarter?**

	✔
cutting over absorbed £400; finishing over absorbed £600	
cutting over absorbed £400; finishing under absorbed £600	
cutting under absorbed £400; finishing under absorbed £600	
cutting under absorbed £400; finishing over absorbed £600	

Section 2

Task 2.1

Westlake Limited has prepared a forecast for the next quarter for one of its metal components, WL10. This component is produced in batches and the forecast is based on producing and selling 800 batches.

One of the customers of Westlake Limited has indicated that it may be significantly increasing its order level for component WL10 for the next quarter and it appears that activity levels of 1,000 batches and 1,500 batches are feasible.

The semi-variable costs should be calculated using the high/low method. If 2,000 batches are sold the total semi-variable cost will be £2,500 and there is a constant unit variable cost up to this volume.

Complete the table below and calculate the estimated profit per batch of WL10 at the different activity levels.

Batches produced and sold	800	1,000	1,500
	£	£	£
Sales revenue	4,400		
Variable costs:			
• Direct materials	1,200		
• Direct labour	1,000		
• Overheads	320		
Semi-variable costs:	1,600		
• Variable element			
• Fixed element			
Total cost	4,120		
Total profit	280		
Profit per batch (to 2 decimal places)	0.35		

Task 2.2

Westlake Limited makes a product which is coded WL15. The selling price of product WL15 is £24 per unit and the total variable cost is £16 per unit. Westlake Limited estimates that the fixed costs per quarter associated with this product are £1,760.

(a)   **Calculate the budgeted breakeven, in units, for product WL15.**

units

(b)   **Calculate the budgeted breakeven, in £, for product WL15.**

£

(c)   **Complete the table below to show the budgeted margin of safety in units, and the margin of safety percentage if Westlake Limited sells 400 units or 500 units of product WL15.**

Units of WL15 sold	400	500
Margin of safety (units)		
Margin of safety (percentage)		

(d)   **If Westlake Limited wishes to make a profit of £2,400, how many units of WL15 must it sell?**

units

(e)   **If Westlake Limited reduces the selling price of WL15 by £1, what will be the impact on the breakeven point and the margin of safety, assuming no change in the number of units sold?**

	✔
The breakeven point will decrease and the margin of safety will increase.	
The breakeven point will stay the same but the margin of safety will decrease.	
The breakeven point will decrease and the margin of safety will stay the same.	
The breakeven point will increase and the margin of safety will decrease.	

Task 2.3

The cutting department of Westlake Limited uses process costing for some of its products.

One particular product product is made in two production processes. The process 1 account and the process 2 account for December for this product have been partly completed but the following information is also relevant:

- Westlake Limited expects a normal loss of 10% during process 1, which it then sells for scrap at 20p per kg

- Westlake Limited expects a normal loss of 5% during process 2, which is then sells for scrap at 60p per kg

(a)   Complete the process 1 account below for December.

Process 1 Account							
Description	**kg**	**Unit cost £**	**Total cost £**	**Description**	**kg**	**Unit cost £**	**Total cost £**
Material M10	1,000	0.50		Normal loss		0.20	
Labour			400	Transfer to			
Overheads			200	process 2	900	1.20	

(b)   Complete the process 2 account below for December.

Process 2 Account							
Description	**kg**	**Unit cost £**	**Total cost £**	**Description**	**kg**	**Unit cost £**	**Total cost £**
Transfer from				Normal loss		0.60	
process 1	900			Output	830		
Labour			180	Abnormal loss			
Overheads			135				

Task 2.4

Westlake Limited has the following original budget and actual performance for product WL18 for the year ending 31 December.

	budget	actual
Volume sold	3,000	3,240
	£	£
Sales revenue	19,500	20,100
Less costs:		
Direct materials	5,500	5,800
Direct labour	4,300	4,900
Overheads	6,700	7,100
Operating profit	3,000	2,300

Both direct materials and direct labour are variable costs, but the overheads are fixed.

Complete the table below to show a flexed budget and the resulting variances against this budget for the year. Show the actual variance amount, for sales and each cost, in the column headed 'Variance' and indicate whether this is Favourable or Adverse by entering F or A in the final column. If neither F nor A, enter 0.

	Flexed budget	Actual	Variance	Favourable (F) or Adverse (A)
Volume sold		3,240		
	£	£	£	
Sales revenue		20,100		
Less costs:				
Direct materials		5,800		
Direct labour		4,900		
Overheads		7,100		
Operating profit		2,300		

Task 2.5

One of the machines in the cutting department is nearing the end of its working life and Westlake Limited is considering purchasing a replacement machine.

Estimates have been made for the initial capital cost, sales income and operating costs of the replacement machine, which is expected to have a working life of three years, at the end of which it will be sold for £6,000:

	Year 0 £000	Year 1 £000	Year 2 £000	Year 3 £000
Capital expenditure	40			
Disposal				6
Other cash flows:				
Sales revenue		33	40	35
Operating costs		12	15	14

The company appraises capital investment projects using a 10% cost of capital.

(a) **Complete the table below and calculate the net present value of the proposed replacement machine (to the nearest £000).**

	Year 0 £000	Year 1 £000	Year 2 £000	Year 3 £000
Capital expenditure				
Disposal				
Sales revenue				
Operating costs				
Net cash flows				
PV factors	1.0000	0.9091	0.8264	0.7513
Discounted cash flows				
Net present value				

Tick to show if the net present value is

positive	
or negative	

(b) **Calculate the payback period of the proposed replacement machine to the nearest whole month.**

The payback period is _____ year(s) and _____ months.

Costs and revenues

Practice assessment 2

This Assessment is based on a sample assessment provided by the AAT and is reproduced here with their kind permission.

Section 1

Task 1.1

The following information is available for plastic grade XL5:

- Annual demand – 62,500 kilograms.
- Annual holding cost per kilogram – £1
- Fixed ordering cost – £2

(a) Calculate the Economic Order Quantity (EOQ) for XL5

The inventory record shown below for plastic grade XL5 for the month of December has only been fully completed for the first three weeks of the month.

(b) Complete the entries in the inventory record for the two receipts on 24 and 28 December that were ordered using the EOQ method.

(c) Complete ALL entries in the inventory record for the two issues in the month and for the closing balance at the end of December using the AVCO method of issuing inventory.

Show the costs per kilogram (kg) in £ to 3 decimal places, and the total costs in whole £.

Inventory record for plastic grade XL5

Date	Receipts			Issues			Balance	
	Quantity (kg)	Cost per kg (£)	Total cost (£)	Quantity (kg)	Cost per kg (£)	Total cost (£)	Quantity (kg)	Total cost (£)
Balance as at 22 December							110	132
24 December		1.298						
26 December				300				
28 December		1.302						
30 December				400				

Task 1.2

Drag and drop the correct entries into the Journal below to record the following FOUR accounting transactions:

1.   Receipt of plastic components into inventory paying on credit.

2.   Issue of plastic components from inventory to production.

3.   Receipt of plastic components into inventory paying immediately by BACS.

4.   Return of plastic components from production to inventory.

The drag and drop choices are:

■   Dr. Bank, Cr. Inventory

■   Dr. Trade Payables' Control, Cr. Inventory

■   Dr. Inventory, Cr. Bank

■   Dr. Inventory, Cr. Trade Payables' Control

■   Dr. Inventory, Cr. Production

■   Dr. Production, Cr. Inventory

	Drag and drop choice
Transaction 1	
Transaction 2	
Transaction 3	
Transaction 4	

Task 1.3

Below is a weekly timesheet for one of Broadsword Ltd's employees, who is paid as follows:

- For a basic six-hour shift every day from Monday to Friday – basic pay.

- For any overtime in excess of the basic six hours, on any day from Monday to Friday – the extra hours are paid at time-and-a-half (basic pay plus an overtime premium equal to half of basic pay).

- For three contracted hours each Saturday morning – basic pay.

- For any hours in excess of three hours on Saturday – the extra hours are paid at double time (basic pay plus an overtime premium equal to basic pay).

- For any hours worked on Sunday – paid at double time (basic pay plus an overtime premium equal to basic pay).

Complete the columns headed Basic pay, Overtime premium and Total pay.

(Notes: Zero figures should be entered in cells where appropriate; Overtime pay is the premium amount paid for the extra hours worked).

Employee's weekly timesheet for week ending 7 December

Employee: D. Boy			Profit Centre: Plastic extrusion			
Employee number: P450			Basic pay per hour: £12.00			
	Hours spent on production	*Hours worked on indirect work*	*Notes*	*Basic pay (£)*	*Overtime premium (£)*	*Total pay (£)*
Monday	6	2	10am-12am cleaning of machinery			
Tuesday	2	4	9am-1pm customer care course			
Wednesday	8					
Thursday	6					
Friday	6	1	3-4pm health & safety training			
Saturday	6					
Sunday	3					
Total	**37**	**7**				

Task 1.4

Broadsword Ltd's budgeted overheads for the next financial year are:

	£	£
Depreciation of plant and equipment		804,150
Power for production machinery		715,000
Rent and rates		104,500
Light and heat		23,100
Indirect labour costs:		
Maintenance	101,150	
Stores	36,050	
General Administration	240,100	
Total indirect labour cost		377,300

The following information is also available:

Department	Net book value of plant and equipment	Production machinery power usage (KwH)	Floor space (square metres)	Number of employees
Production centres:				
Plastic moulding	5,600,000	2,145,000		14
Plastic extrusion	2,400,000	1,430,000		10
Support cost centres:				
Maintenance			14,000	5
Stores			8,400	2
General Administration			5,600	7
Total	8,000,000	3,575,000	28,000	38

Overheads are allocated or apportioned on the most appropriate basis. The total overheads of the support cost centres are then reapportioned to the two production centres using the direct method.

▪ 76% of the maintenance cost centre's time is spent maintaining production machinery in the plastic moulding production centre and the remainder in the plastic extrusion production centre.

▪ The stores cost centre makes 60% of its issues to the plastic moulding production centre, and 40% to the plastic extrusion production centre.

▪ General administration supports the two production centres equally.

▪ There is no reciprocal servicing between the three support cost centres.

Complete the apportionment table below using the data on the previous page.

	Basis of apportionment	Plastic moulding (£)	Plastic extrusion (£)	Maintenance (£)	Stores (£)	General Admin (£)	Totals (£)
Depreciation of plant and equipment							
Power for production machinery							
Rent and rates							
Light and heat							
Indirect labour							
Totals							
Reapportion Maintenance							
Reapportion Stores							
Reapportion General Admin							
Total overheads to production centres							

Task 1.5

Next quarter Broadsword Ltd's budgeted overheads and activity levels are:

	Plastic moulding	Plastic extrusion
Budgeted overheads (£)	325,996	178,200
Budgeted direct labour hours	16,300	9,900
Budgeted machine hours	5,258	3,300

(a) What would be the budgeted overhead absorption rate for each department if this were set based on their both being heavily automated? ✓

(a)	Plastic moulding £20/hour, Plastic extrusion £18/hour	
(b)	Plastic moulding £20/hour, Plastic extrusion £54/hour	
(c)	Plastic moulding £62/hour, Plastic extrusion £18/hour	
(d)	Plastic moulding £62/hour, Plastic extrusion £54/hour	

(b) What would be the budgeted overhead absorption rate for each department if this were set based on their both being labour intensive? ✓

(a)	Plastic moulding £20/hour, Plastic extrusion £18/hour	
(b)	Plastic moulding £20/hour, Plastic extrusion £54/hour	
(c)	Plastic moulding £62/hour, Plastic extrusion £18/hour	
(d)	Plastic moulding £62/hour, Plastic extrusion £54/hour	

Additional data

At the end of the quarter actual overheads incurred were found to be:

	Plastic moulding	Plastic extrusion
Actual overheads (£)	315,906	198,100

(c) Assuming that exactly the same amount of overheads was absorbed as budgeted, what were the budgeted under or over absorptions in the quarter? ✓

(a)	Plastic moulding over absorbed £10,090 Plastic extrusion over absorbed £19,900	
(b)	Plastic moulding over absorbed £10,090 Plastic extrusion under absorbed £19,900	
(c)	Plastic moulding under absorbed £10,090 Plastic extrusion under absorbed £19,900	
(d)	Plastic moulding under absorbed £10,090 Plastic extrusion over absorbed £19,900	

Section 2

Task 2.1

Broadsword Ltd has prepared a forecast for the next quarter for one of its small plastic components, ZY24. This component is produced in batches and the forecast is based on selling and producing 1,200 batches.

One of the customers of Broadsword Ltd has indicated that it may be significantly increasing its order level for component ZY24 for the next quarter and it appears that activity levels of 1,500 batches and 2,000 batches are feasible.

The semi-variable costs should be calculated using the high-low method. If 3,000 batches are sold the total semi-variable cost will be £7,380, and there is a constant unit variable cost up to this volume.

Complete the table below and calculate the estimated profit per batch of ZY24 at the different activity levels.

Batches produced and sold	1,200 £	1,500 £	2,000 £
Sales revenue	36,000		
Variable costs:			
■ Direct materials	5,400		
■ Direct labour	12,600		
■ Overheads	7,200		
Semi-variable costs:	3,780		
■ Variable element			
■ Fixed element			
Total cost	28,980		
Total profit	7,020		
Profit per batch (to 2 decimal places)	5.85		

Task 2.2

Product TR28 has a selling price of £23 per unit with a total variable cost of £15 per unit. Broadsword Ltd estimates that the fixed costs per quarter associated with this product are £36000.

(a) Calculate the budgeted breakeven, in units, for product TR28.

units

(b) Calculate the budgeted breakeven, in £, for product TR28.

£

(c) Complete the table below to show the budgeted margin of safety in units, and the margin of safety percentage if Broadsword Ltd sells 5000 units or 6000 units of product TR28.

Units of TR28 sold	5000	6000
	£	£
Margin of safety (units)		
Margin of safety percentage		

(d) If Broadsword Ltd wishes to make a profit of £20,000, how many units of TR28 must it sell?

units

(e) If Broadsword Ltd increases the selling price of TR28 by £1, what will be the impact on the breakeven point and the margin of safety, assuming no change in the number of units sold?

✓

(a)	The breakeven point will decrease and the margin of safety will increase.	
(b)	The breakeven point will stay the same but the margin of safety will decrease.	
(c)	The breakeven point will decrease and the margin of safety will stay the same.	
(d)	The breakeven point will increase and the margin of safety will decrease.	

Task 2.3

The Plastic extrusion department of Broadsword Ltd uses process costing for some of its products.

The process account for December for one particular process has been partly completed but the following information is also relevant:

■ Two employees worked on this process during December. Each employee worked 40 hours per week for 4 weeks and was paid £10 per hour.

■ Overheads are absorbed on the basis of £16 per labour hour.

■ Broadsword Ltd expects a normal loss of 5% during this process, which it then sells for scrap at 60p per kg.

(a) Complete the process account below for December.

Description	kg	Unit cost (£)	Total cost (£)	Description	kg	Unit cost (£)	Total cost (£)
Material XG4	600	1.20		Normal loss		0.60	
Material XH3	400	1.50		Output	1330		
Material XJ9	400	0.61					
Labour							
Overheads							

(b) Identify the correct entry for each of the following in a process account.

	Debit	Credit
Abnormal loss		
Abnormal gain		

Task 2.4

Broadsword Ltd has the following original budget and actual performance for product ZT4 for the year ending 31 December.

	Budget	Actual
Volume sold	100,000	144,000
	£000	£000
Sales revenue	2,000	3,600
Less costs:		
Direct materials	350	530
Direct labour	400	480
Overheads	980	1,228
Operating profit	270	1,362

Both direct materials and direct labour are variable costs, but the overheads are fixed

Complete the table below to show a flexed budget and the resulting variances against this budget for the year. Show the actual variance amount, for sales and each cost, in the column headed 'Variance' and indicate whether this is Favourable or Adverse by entering F or V in the final column. If neither F nor V, enter 0.

	Flexed Budget	Actual	Variance	Favourable (F) or Adverse (A)
Volume sold		144,000		
	£000	£000	£000	
Sales revenue		3,600		
Less costs:				
Direct materials		530		
Direct labour		480		
Overheads		1,228		
Operating profit		1,362		

Task 2.5

One of the extrusion machines in the Plastic extrusion department is nearing the end of its working life and Broadsword Ltd is considering purchasing a replacement machine.

Estimates have been made for the initial capital cost, sales income and operating costs of the replacement machine, which is expected to have a working life of three years:

	Year 0 £000	Year 1 £000	Year 2 £000	Year 3 £000
Capital expenditure	900			
Other cash flows:				
Sales income		420	560	800
Operating costs		120	150	190

The company appraises capital investment projects using a 15% cost of capital.

(a) Complete the table below and calculate the net present value of the proposed replacement machine (to the nearest £000).

	Year 0 £000	Year 1 £000	Year 2 £000	Year 3 £000
Capital expenditure				
Sales income				
Operating costs				
Net cash flows				
PV factors	1.0000	0.8696	0.7561	0.6575
Discounted cash flows				
Net present value				

The net present value is **positive / negative**.

(b) Calculate the payback of the proposed replacement machine to the nearest whole month.

The payback period is . . . . Year(s) and . . . . Months

Practice assessment answers

Section 1

Task 1.1

(a)

EOQ = 400 kg

Tutorial note:

$$\sqrt{\frac{2 \times 16,000 \times 20}{4}}$$

(b) and (c)

Inventory record for metal grade M5

Date	Receipts			Issues			Balance	
	Quantity (kg)	Cost per kg	Total Cost	Quantity (kg)	Cost per kg	Total Cost	Quantity (kg)	Total Cost
		£	£		£	£		£
Balance as at 22 December							350	840
23 December	400	2.50	1,000				350 400 750	840 1,000 1,840
28 December				350 150 500	2.40 2.50	840 375 1,215	250	625
29 December	400	2.60	1,040				250 400 650	625 1,040 1,665
30 December				250 50 300	2.50 2.60	625 130 755	350	910

Task 1.2

Transaction	Account debited	Account credited
1. Paid wages of direct labour employees	Production	Wages control
2. Paid wages of factory supervisors	Production overheads	Wages control
3. Paid wages of office staff	Non-production overheads	Wages control
4. Correction of wages overpaid in error to factory supervisors	Wages control	Production overheads

Task 1.3

Employee: S Wong			Profit Centre: Cutting			
Employee number: HZ24			Basic pay per hour: £14.00			
	Hours spent on production	Hours worked on indirect work	Notes	Basic pay £	Overtime premium £	Total pay £
Monday	6	0		84	0	84
Tuesday	6	2	8 am -10 am maintenance	112	14	126
Wednesday	7	0		98	7	105
Thursday	4	3	9 am -12 noon training	98	7	105
Friday	7	1	2 pm - 3 pm first aid course	112	14	126
Saturday	4	0		56	14	70
Sunday	2	0		28	28	56
Total	36	6		588	84	672

Task 1.4

	Basis of apportionment	Cutting £	Finishing £	Maintenance £	Stores £	Admin £	Totals £
Depreciation of production machinery	NBV/carrying amount of machinery	2,670	1,780				4,450
Power for production machinery	Power usage of machinery	2,376	594				2,970
Rent and rates	Floor space			1,995	3,420	3,135	8,550
Light and heat	Floor space			525	900	825	2,250
Indirect labour	Allocated			16,400	30,300	35,650	82,350
Totals		5,046	2,374	18,920	34,620	39,610	100,570
Reapportion Maintenance		15,136	3,784	(18,920)			
Reapportion Stores		24,234	10,386		(34,620)		
Reapportion Administration		19,805	19,805			(39,610)	
Total overheads to production centres		64,221	36,349				100,570

Task 1.5

(a)   cutting £9 per hour; finishing £10 per hour

(b)   cutting £14 per hour; finishing £11 per hour

(c)   cutting under absorbed £400; finishing over absorbed £600

Section 2

Task 2.1

Batches produced and sold	800	1,000	1,500
	£	£	£
Sales revenue	4,400	5,500	8,250
Variable costs:			
• Direct materials	1,200	1,500	2,250
• Direct labour	1,000	1,250	1,875
• Overheads	320	400	600
Semi-variable costs:	1,600		
• Variable element		750	1,125
• Fixed element		1,000	1,000
Total cost	4,120	4,900	6,850
Total profit	280	600	1,400
Profit per batch (to 2 decimal places)	0.35	0.60	0.93

Task 2.2

(a) | 220 units |

(b) | £5,280 |

(c)

Units of WL15 sold	400	500
Margin of safety (units)	180	280
Margin of safety (percentage)	45	56

(d) | 520 units |

(e)   The breakeven point will increase and the margin of safety will decrease.

Task 2.3

(a)

Process 1 Account							
Description	**kg**	**Unit cost £**	**Total cost £**	**Description**	**kg**	**Unit cost £**	**Total cost £**
Material M10	1,000	0.50	500	Normal loss	100	0.20	20
Labour			400	Transfer to			
Overheads			200	process 2	900	1.20	1,080
	1,000		1,100		1,000		1,100

(b)

Process 2 Account							
Description	**kg**	**Unit cost £**	**Total cost £**	**Description**	**kg**	**Unit cost £**	**Total cost £**
Transfer from				Normal loss	45	0.60	27
process 1	900	1.20	1,080	Output	830	1.60	1,328
Labour			180	Abnormal loss	25	1.60	40
Overheads			135				
	900		1,395		900		1,395

Task 2.4

	Flexed budget	Actual	Variance	Favourable (F) or Adverse (A)
Volume sold	3,240	3,240		
	£	£	£	
Sales revenue	21,060	20,100	960	A
Less costs:				
Direct materials	5,940	5,800	140	F
Direct labour	4,644	4,900	256	A
Overheads	6,700	7,100	400	A
Operating profit	3,776	2,300	1,476	A

Task 2.5

(a)

	Year 0 £000	Year 1 £000	Year 2 £000	Year 3 £000
Capital expenditure	(40)			
Disposal				6
Sales revenue		33	40	35
Operating costs		12	15	14
Net cash flows	(40)	21	25	27
PV factors	1.0000	0.9091	0.8264	0.7513
Discounted cash flows	(40)	19	21	20
Net present value	20			

	positive	✔
or	negative	

(b) The payback period is 1 year(s) and 9 months.

Answers to Practice Assessment 2

Section 1

Task 1.1

(a) The EOQ is 500kg = $\sqrt{\dfrac{2 \times 62{,}500 \times 2}{1}}$

(b) and (c)

Date	Receipts Quantity (kg)	Receipts Cost per kg (£)	Receipts Total cost (£)	Issues Quantity (kg)	Issues Cost per kg (£)	Issues Total cost (£)	Balance Quantity (kg)	Balance Total cost (£)
Balance as at 22 December							110	132
24 December	500	1.298	649				610	781
26 December				300	1.280	384	310	397
28 December	500	1.302	651				810	1048
30 December				400	1.294	518	410	530

Task 1.2

Transaction 1	Dr. Inventory, Cr. Trade payables' Control
Transaction 2	Dr. Production, Cr. Inventory
Transaction 3	Dr. Inventory, Cr. Bank
Transaction 4	Dr. Inventory, Cr. Production

Task 1.3

Employee: D. Boy			**Profit Centre:** Plastic extrusion			
Employee number: P450			**Basic pay per hour:** £12.00			
	Hours spent on production	Hours worked on indirect work	Notes	Basic pay (£)	Overtime premium (£)	Total pay (£)
Monday	6	2	10am-12am cleaning of machinery	96	12	108
Tuesday	2	4	9am-1pm customer care course	72	–	72
Wednesday	8			96	12	108
Thursday	6			72	–	72
Friday	6	1	3-4pm health and safety training	84	6	90
Saturday	6			72	36	108
Sunday*	3			–	72	72
Total	**37**	**7**		**492**	**138**	**630**

Task 1.4

	Basis of apportionment	Plastic moulding (£)	Plastic extrusion (£)	Maintenance (£)	Stores (£)	General Admin (£)	Totals (£)
Dep'n of plant & equipment	NBV of plant and equipment	562,905	241,245				804,150
Power for production machinery	Production machinery power usage (KwH)	429,000	286,000				715,000
Rent and rates	Floor space			52,250	31,350	20,900	104,500
Light and heat	Floor space			11,550	6,930	4,620	23,100
Indirect labour	Allocated			101,150	36,050	240,100	377,300
Totals		991,905	527,245	164,950	74,330	265,620	2,024,050
Reapportion Maintenance		125,362	39,588	(164,950)			
Reapportion Stores		44,598	29,732		(74,330)		
Reapportion General Admin		132,810	132,810			(265,620)	
Total overheads to production centres		1,294,675	729,375				2,024,050

Task 1.5

(a)   The correct answer is (d).

(b)   The correct answer is (a).

(c)   The correct answer is (b).

Section 2

Task 2.1

Batches produced and sold	1,200	1,500	2,000
	£	£	£
Sales revenue	36,000	45,000	60,000
Variable costs:			
▦ Direct materials	5,400	6,750	9,000
▦ Direct labour	12,600	15,750	21,000
▦ Overheads	7,200	9,000	12,000
Semi-variable costs:	3,780		
▦ Variable element		3,000	4,000
▦ Fixed element		1,380	1,380
Total cost	28,980	35,880	47,380
Total profit	7,020	9,120	12,620
Profit per batch (to 2 decimal places)	5.85	6.08	6.31

Task 2.2

(a)   4,500 units

(b)   £103,500

(c)

Units of TR 28 sold	5,000	6,000
	£	£
Margin of safety (units)	500	1,500
Margin of safety percentage	10%	25%

(d)   7,000 units

(e)   The correct answer is (a).

Task 2.3 (a)

Description	kg	Unit cost (£)	Total cost (£)	Description	kg	Unit cost (£)	Total cost (£)
Material XG4	600	1.20	720	Normal loss	70	0.60	42
Material XH3	400	1.50	600	Output	1,330	7.40	9,842
Material XJ9	400	0.61	244				
Labour			3,200				
Overheads			5,120				
	1,400		9,884		1,400		9,884

(b) Abnormal loss   *Credit*

       Abnormal gain   *Debit*

Task 2.4

	Flexed Budget	Actual	Variance	Favourable (F) or Adverse (A)
Volume sold	144,000	144,000		
	£000	£000	£000	
Sales revenue	2,880	3,600	720	F
Less costs:				
Direct materials	504	530	26	A
Direct labour	576	480	96	F
Overheads	980	1,228	248	A
Operating profit	820	1,362	542	F

Task 2.5

(a)

	Year 0 £000	Year 1 £000	Year 2 £000	Year 3 £000
Capital expenditure	(900)			
Sales income		420	560	800
Operating costs		120	150	190
Net cash flows	(900)	300	410	610
PV factors	1.0000	0.8696	0.7561	0.6575
Discounted cash flows	(900)	261	310	401
Net present value	72			

The net present value is **positive**.

(b)   The payback period is 2 Years and 4 Months

The Sheffield College

Norton LRC
Telephone: 0114 260 2334